CHILDREN'S
LITERATURE
of the
ENGLISH
RENAISSANCE

CHILDREN'S LITERATURE

of the

ENGLISH RENAISSANCE

Warren W. Wooden

Edited, with an introduction, by

JEANIE WATSON

THE UNIVERSITY PRESS OF KENTUCKY

Copyright © 1986 by The University Press of Kentucky

Scholarly publisher for the Commonwealth,
serving Bellarmine College, Berea College, Centre
College of Kentucky,Eastern Kentucky University,
The Filson Club, Georgetown College, Kentucky
Historical Society, Kentucky State University,
Morehead State University, Murray State University,
Northern Kentucky University, Transylvania University,
University of Kentucky, University of Louisville,
and Western Kentucky University.

Editorial and Sales Offices: Lexington, Kentucky 40506-0024

Library of Congress Cataloging-in-Publication Data

Wooden, Warren W.
    Children's literature of the English Renaisannce.

    Some essays published previously.
    Bibliography: p.
    Includes index.
    Contents: From Caxton to Comenius—Childermass
sermons in late medieval England—Childhood and
death—[etc.]
    1. Children's literature, English—History and
criticism.   2. English literature—Early modern, 1500-
1700—History and criticism.   3. Children—England—
Books and reading—History.   I. Watson, Jeanie,
1943-   II. Title.
PR990.W6   1986   820'.9'9282   86-15651
ISBN 0-8131-1587-6

Contents

Acknowledgments

John T. Shawcross has been an equal partner in readying this collection of essays for publication, giving generously of his time and experience. Like Woody himself, John is a scholar and a gentleman and an encourager of the work of other scholars; his participation in this project has, therefore, seemed most appropriate. I am deeply grateful for his warm support.

I would also like to acknowledge the assistance of the King Library of the University of Kentucky in obtaining the illustrations. And, finally, I wish to thank the following for permission to republish articles: *Bulletin of the West Virginia Association of College English Teachers*, the Children's Literature Association, Duke University Press, and *Fifteenth Century Studies*.

JEANIE WATSON

Introduction

Warren W. Wooden died 27 December 1983. Though he was only forty-two, he was already a Renaissance scholar of note and a critic to be reckoned with, specifically in the study of Thomas More and John Foxe and, more generally, in the several diverse areas of Tudor and Stuart English literature: biography, hagiography, iconography, popular culture, and the rhetorical strategies employed by poets, politicians, and sermonizers. Weaving its way through these early and primary interests in ever-clearer and more distinct patterns was his inquiry into the origins of English children's literature. Children's literature came to be the scholarly concern closest to his heart and the one, I believe, that was stitching together the various fabrics of his talent.

When he died, Woody was at work on a full-scale study to be titled "The Origins of Children's Literature in England, ca. 1500-1700: A Critical Investigation and Survey." There is at present no such comprehensive treatment of children's literature during this period, a task that requires first a thorough grounding in Renaissance literature and culture. As Woody says in his last essay: "The researcher investigating the historical roots of children's literature needs to look back to the works written for a general audience of readers during the Renaissance, books and pamphlets whose appeal was inclusive and eclectic." The diversity of his own research and scholarship uniquely prepared him to write the book he envisioned. He had received support for the project from the Children's Literature Association and the American Philosophical Society and a senior research fellowship for 1983-84 from the American Council of Learned Societies. I want here to quote at length from Woody's ACLS fellowship proposal because the proposal indicates the scope of the work that needs to be done in the field and suggests a structure for that work. In addition, it provides a context for the essays in this volume, since the whole cloth of the proposed book is woven from the individual threads of research manifested by these essays. He writes:

I intend to investigate the origins of English children's literature from the introduction of printing in England through the conclusion of the seventeenth century with the aim of producing a comprehensive, book-length manuscript exploring the cross-currents of this rich but neglected area. Although individual articles and chapters of such larger studies as Percy Muir's *English Children's Books, 1600-1900* (1954), F.J. Harvey Darton's classic *Children's Books in England: Five Centuries of Social Life* (2nd ed., 1958), and Mary F. Thwaite's *From Primer to Pleasure in Reading: An Introduction to the History of Children's Books in England* (1963) survey aspects of the subject, there is no full-scale treatment of children's literature during its formative period in England. Perhaps the nearest approach to a comprehensive treatment is William Sloane's *Children's Books in England and America in the Seventeenth Century* (1955), a valuable combination history and annotated checklist. Yet Sloane's definition of a children's book as a book "written for children only" so restricts his survey as to create a misleading impression of what Renaissance English children actually read. Thus, while many seventeenth century children were certainly subjected to the Puritan tracts and various godly instructional manuals aimed at them and catalogued by Sloane, the children also made their way into the literary marketplace and devoured the chapbook adventure stories, popular ballads, and fairy lore provided for audiences of all ages by enterprising English printers. Thus, a larger view is wanted, one which recognizes, as Margaret C. Gillespie emphasizes, that "the world of children's literature *has been* and *continues to be* one that is dominated by children's choices" (*Literature for Children: History and Trends*, 1970); consequently, Sheila Egoff's definition of a children's book is far more apt and functional, especially for the early period: "In the true sense, a children's book is simply one in which a child finds pleasure" (*The Republic of Childhood*, 1967). The study I propose, then, will examine not only the books written specifically for children during the English Renaissance but also the works children selected from the bookstalls, their parents' libraries, and their playmates' collections and made their own.

It is a critical commonplace that during the medieval period the audiences of literature are differentiated by social class or status rather than by age. While some works, such as Chaucer's *Treatise on the Astrolabe* written for his ten-year-old son, Lewis, or *The Babee's Book* (ca. 1475), were written specifically for a youthful audience, most English children enjoyed with their elders the rich oral tradition of medieval literature—the ballads, Corpus Christi drama, and popularized *chansons de geste* that flourished during the fifteenth century. When William Caxton set up his press at the sign of the Red Pole in Westminster late in the century, he soon made far more widely accessible many of the most popular works of the era. Some of Caxton's books had particular reference to children; for example, the *Book of Curtesye* (1477) taught the young male reader how to behave in a noble household, while girls were served by *The Knight of the Tower* (1484), a gentleman's instructions to his daughter. Meanwhile, children delighted in Caxton's *Fables of Aesop* (1483) and such chivalric romances as Malory's *Le Morte D'Arthur* (1485).

With the beginning of Caxton's publishing enterprise, we can see specific types of literature for children emerging in print. The instructional manuals, primarily courtesy books, remain popular (though doubtless more so with adult purchasers than with child readers), leading in a secular direction through such works as

Robert Whittington's translation of Erasmus's *A Lytell Booke of Good Manners for Chyldren* (1532), Hugh Rhodes's *Boke of Nurture* (1545), and Francis Seager's *The Schoole of Vertue and Booke of good Nourture for Chyldren to learn theyr Dutie by* (1557). At a somewhat later date, under the impetus especially of evangelical Protestantism, a flood of religious handbooks and tracts issued from the presses to guide little feet on the path to heaven. While the goal of salvation is a common one, children's books in the religious category differ markedly in their approach, one type seeking to frighten the child away from sin (e.g., James Janeway's *A Token for Children*, 1672, and Thomas White's *A Little Book for Little Children*, 1674), another seeking to lure him to heaven through delightful instruction in godly behavior (e.g., William Jole's *The Father's Blessing*, 1674, and John Bunyan's *A Book for Boys and Girls*, 1686). This religious tradition of didactic literature for children needs to be reassessed, in particular, to determine its relationship to two Renaissance masterpieces, Foxe's *Book of Martyrs* (1563) and Bunyan's *Pilgrim's Progress* (1678), works that blend Christian instruction with riveting narratives children found irresistible. Few critics are aware, for example, that Foxe specifically addresses children on numerous occasions in the *Book of Martyrs*, calling their attention to positive and negative examples of childish conduct and referring them to the graphic woodcuts adjoined to the text.

While the English humanists and educators applauded the production of instructional manuals and school texts for boys, they were acutely aware that children's reading was by no means confined to such materials. Particular targets of their ire were the popular chivalric romances emerging from Caxton's press and those of his fellow printers, such as Wynken de Worde's *A Lytell Geste of Robin Hode* (ca. 1500) and Richard Pynson's *Guy of Warwick* (ca. 1500). Educators inveighed against these adventure stories, condemning their "open mans slaughter and bold bawdry" (Roger Ascham, *The Scholemaster*, 1570), warning parents that children must be kept "from reading of fayned fables, vayne fantasies, and wanton stories and songs of love, which bring mischiefe to youth" (Hugh Rhodes, *Boke of Nurture*, 1545), and deploring the general plague of "idle books . . . fables, love songs, baudry ballads, heathen husks, youth's poison" (Zachary Boyd, *Petition to the General Assembly of Scotland*, 1644). Here begin the attempts to [censor] and restrict children's reading matter; however, the educators' assault served only to drive the romances underground, out of the classrooms and into the pockets of schoolboys and bedchambers of girls. The spread of chapbook printing from the continent to England in the sixteenth century enormously facilitated this process through stripped down, inexpensive versions of the old romances, little books which found their way into the households of even the poorest English families. Thus John Bunyan confesses to having read in his youth "George on Horseback" and "Sir Bevis of Southhampton"; and Bunyan's reading habits were more typical than his guilt about them. Through the medium of the chapbook and broadside in sixteenth and seventeenth century England, Tom Thumb, the fairies, the Babes in the Wood, and a torrent of fascinating stories became available to the youthful reader.

Caxton is the fountainhead of yet another popular type of Renaissance children's literature: the beast fable. While the collection of tales gathered under the rubric of *Aesop's Fables* was not written specifically for children, their attraction to children and evident utility as a school text made Aesop a staple of medieval education. The humanists continued this enthusiasm for Aesop especially because, as Sir Thomas Elyot pointed out in *The Book Named the Governor* (1531), the fables were a splendid way to introduce Greek language and literature, one of the humanist reformers' favorite subjects. Caxton's English version of *Reynard the Fox* appeared in 1481, and the beast fable, perhaps the most universal of all literature for children, was well established in Renaissance England. The various permutations and progeny of the beast fable in Renaissance England down through the talking animals of nursery rhymes and ballads have never been adequately mapped. Nor has the relation of such works as John Taylor's *A Dogge of Warre* (1628), the great-grandfather of the Lassie stories, to the tradition of beast stories been considered.

There is more, much more, to be explored in the survey I

propose. The illustrated children's book, for example, develops at this period, in a line which runs from the woodcuts of Caxton's *Aesop* through the vivid engravings of Foxe's *Book of Martyrs* to the mid-seventeenth century translation of Comenius's *Orbis Sensualium Pictus* (1659). And the springs of English nonsense verse for children are to be found in John Taylor's popular *Nonsense upon Sence, or Sence upon Nonsence* (ca. 1653). My study will mine the riches of English Renaissance literature, including both works written for children and those appropriated or "adopted" by children, with the hope of establishing a canon of children's literature from the invention of printing down to 1700. Within the canon, I will differentiate specific types of children's literature, studying the contours and constituents of each class to illustrate that most of the varieties of literature we today regularly associate with children arose during the Renaissance. If I succeed in this task, my study should call for a re-examination of the origin of English children's literature and re-direct the attention of teachers and scholars to the early period as an abundant storehouse of lively children's literature rather than a barren wasteland pockmarked by dreary didactic tracts.

The proposal itself indicates directions for research in the field of early children's literature, and Woody's written work contributes significantly to that research. Some of the articles in this collection extend the boundaries of the existing canon of early English children's literature, in the way that the proposal anticipates. Others deal with the criteria for inclusion in the canon and with the cultural, pedagogical, political, and theological realities of Renaissance society that ought to be taken into account when considering the literary works. What are the Renaissance roots of children's literature, and where does one look for them? What is the place of children's literature in literary history? What does the literature tell us about the nature of childhood in the Renaissance?

The essays in this volume are arranged chronologically by subject matter, beginning with the article "From Caxton to Comenius: The Origins of Children's Literature," originally presented at the International Fifteenth Century Symposium at the University of Regensburg, West Germany (August 1982). This essay concentrates on the stages of evolution and development in illustrated books for children in England by looking at three key works the Renaissance thought particularly appropriate for children: William Caxton's *Fables of Aesop* (1483), John Foxe's *Book of Martyrs* (1563), and the *Orbis Pictus* of the Moravian minister John Amos Comenius, published in 1657 (with an English translation in 1658 by the schoolmaster Charles Hoole). Woody argues that children were at least part of the intended audience for the books and that "taken together, the three suggest a comprehensive range of picture-text coordination and use of iconic and realistic illustration for young readers."

A paper on early English children's sermons delivered at the conference on the Literary Aspects of Children's Literature in Savannah, Georgia (June 1978), and the Carolinas Symposium on British Studies at Myrtle Beach, South Carolina (October 1978), was published as "Childermass Ceremonies in Late Medieval England: The Literary Legacy." Here, Woody's purpose is to assess the literary and historical importance of the Boy Bishop sermons, putting them first in their original medieval and early Renaissance setting of religious ceremony. This purpose leads to questions of authorship, audience, the rhetorical strategies of the sermons themselves, and their place in the literary history of the late Middle Ages in England—all of which leads to further questions about the nature of childhood in the period.

In a paper on Skelton's *Philip Sparrow*, delivered at the Children's Literature Discussion Circle at the South Atlantic

Modern Language Association in Washington, D.C. (November 1977), and subsequently published as "Childhood and Death: A Reading of John Skelton's *Philip Sparrow*," Woody shows how Skelton uses medieval and classical antecedents to write a "serious poem about childhood and a poem designed to appeal, on at least one level, to the juvenile reader." The article thus broadens the discussion of literary form as a context for works of children's literature to consider also biographical and sociohistorical issues as part of that context. In *Philip Sparrow*, Skelton explores the "psychic mechanism by which a sensitive child withstands and finally conquers the cruelty of death," and he does so, Woody argues, with a "fidelity to the truths of childhood experience [that] is no less impressive than moving."

"The Topos of Childhood in Marian England" is an essay that grew out of a paper presented at the Modern Language Association meeting in San Francisco (December 1979), in a section on mid-Tudor literature. In this essay, Woody's interest in the metaphoric use of childhood—or "childship"—comes to the fore as he discusses the sixteenth century's interest in the child as "creature and symbol," a Renaissance interest which arose from a complex of factors—pedagogical, theological, social, and political. Within this context, Woody extends and carries out the implications of the article on Childermass Ceremonies, using the Boy Bishops as the prime example.

"John Foxe's *Book of Martyrs* and the Child Reader" was originally presented at the Children's Literature Association in Gainesville, Florida (March 1982). Foxe's massive *Book of Martyrs* (1563), chained as it was to Protestant pulpits for generations and later abridged to make it accessible for the ordinary home library, would have been impossible for the Renaissance child to avoid. The questions that Woody poses have to do with the kind of appeal and psychological effect

Foxe's book had on young readers. More specifically, was Foxe consciusly attempting to reach a juvenile audience, and, if so, what strategies did he use? In other words, is the *Book of Martyrs* "a children's book by design and execution as well as by historical accident"?

Woody first began his work on Renaissance children's literature with the reading of a paper on Drayton's *Nymphidia* at the West Virginia Association of College English Teachers at Jackson's Mill, West Virginia (October 1976). This paper, subsequently published as "Michael Drayton's *Nymphidia*: A Renaissance Children's Classic?" analyzes the elements of the fantasy poem that would have appealed especially to children: the use of native fairy lore and the " 'minifying' technique popularized by Shakespeare's Queen Mab passage." The essay shows that in this mock-heroic poem, by "combining the oral with the literary traditions of the fairy world," Drayton "created a bridge from the oral tradition of native folklore to the great world of European classical literature, a bridge most children of the time were constrained to cross in far more sober vehicles."

Woody's article on Renaissance fairy poetry, "A Child's Garden of Sprites: English Renaissance Fairy Poetry," was delivered at the Modern Language Association in Houston (December 1980). In this essay, he returns to a discussion of fairy tales, the reasons for their popularity in the English Renaissance, and their appropriation by children. He emphasizes, in particular, the "psychological implications of children's fascination with fairyland." The essay also studies the development and direction of English fairy poetry by surveying select representative examples from different literary modes and times: Shakespeare's *A Midsummer Night's Dream*, Jonson's *The Entertainment at Althorpe*, and Drayton's *Nymphidia*, among others.

"The Water-Poet: A Pioneer of Children's Literature,"

Woody's last piece of writing, was scheduled for delivery in the Children's Literature Section at the 1983 Modern Language Association meeting in New York City, a few days after his death. In this paper, within the context of a discussion of the social history of childhood literacy and reading habits, Woody traces the introduction of three types of juvenile literature to a generally forgotten early seventeenth-century author, John Taylor the Water Poet. Taylor, a writer of popular literature, concerned with mass marketing and aware of a potential juvenile audience for non-didactic literature, initiated three types of literature that are today considered important genres of children's literature: simplified miniature redactions of the Bible, or "thumb Bibles"; nonsense verse of the sort later popularized by Lear and Carroll; and animal stories of the faithful animal companion type—a Lassie prototype.

"Nature Moralized: A Reconsideration of John Bunyan's *Country Rhimes for Children* (1686)" was a paper presented at the Children's Literature Division of the Modern Language Association (December 1981). As with the John Taylor piece, its first publication is in this present volume. Bunyan's *Country Rhimes*, one of the first English children's books to aim at entertaining as well as instructing children, is usually given scarcely a footnote in histories of children's literature. Woody's purpose in this essay is to rescue the work and return it to the canon. He accomplishes this by examining the text of the original 1686 edition in terms of the rhetorical strategies and the theological and psychological patternings that structure the book. Given the cultural and religious contexts within which Bunyan wrote, Woody argues that "the conception, design and execution of his children's book is singularly successful in achieving the purpose for which Bunyan wrote it."

There is a central question at the heart of all of these essays: What, exactly, *is* children's literature? This same question, as well as the related ones—What counts as a children's book? What are the criteria for inclusion in the canon? What are the roots of English children's literature and where and how does one look for them?—must figure, even more broadly, in a survey of the origins of children's literature in England. Woody's essays begin to give answers to these questions, sometimes directly and sometimes indirectly through his methodology and the areas he chooses for investigation. His much-reiterated answer to the central definitional question is also the most inclusive one: A literary work becomes a "children's book" when a child finds pleasure in it. Children themselves claim their own literature.

For the most part, Woody's essays deal not with the didactic and pedagogical book overtly and clearly written for children, but with a variety of works not usually considered to be children's books. For this reason, the question of criteria becomes paramount. Since before the eighteenth century there was very little publication of non-academic and non-didactic books for children, children simply read from what was available; they read "adult" literature and appropriated it for their own pleasure. There are two interrelated issues here. First, left to their own discretion, what did children choose to read? Which books were most appealing to them, and what were the sources of the appeal? The second, and overlapping, question is one of author intention. Given the fact that children did read books, it seems reasonable to assume that at least some writers consciously thought of children as a potential audience. How then did this affect their writing strategies? On the bases of what evidence can we assume an author's deliberate appeal to a juvenile audience?

The most obvious place to begin looking for answers is in another question, i.e., to ask an adult what he or she read as a child. There are some adult references to childhood reading and occasionally a mention of the gift of a book, but anecdotal evidence, while conclusive, tends to be sparse and not comprehensive. More inclusive kinds of external evidence come from the book itself. Small size, for example, is a factor that argues for an intended child audience, the assumption being that children delight in small books because they themselves are small and so see the books as belonging to them. Additionally, small books are easier for small hands to hold. A cheap price also argues for child readership. Even an apprentice could afford an occasional chapbook; and since children are often "hard" on books, parents would be more likely to invest in cheap rather than expensive books for them. Illustrations also undoubtedly add to a book's appeal to children. Children love pictures, and pictures hold a child's attention while he or she is being read to and make the child anticipate the next page when reading alone.

There is also the internal evidence of the text to deal with when considering a book's juvenile appeal. Sometimes an author may directly address children within the text of the work, as Foxe does in the *Book of Martyrs*. Further, there are rhetorical strategies available—repetition, comparison, organization, and tone, for example—to draw in a young reader. Most often, however, the writer lets the strategy of appeal extend into the form and genre and subject matter of the literature, counting on these elements of the work to cast their charm. Children read and enjoy books that hold their attention and are easy to read. Children like to be told stories. An exciting narrative with villains, victims, and victors and a suspenseful ending will keep a child reading longer than a sermon full of abstractions. A poem with short lines and enjoyable rhythms that sound repeatedly on the ear and tongue is likely to capture a young reader's attention and give pleasure, especially if the poem is about things in the child's everyday world of dogs and cats and apples and bees—or in his or her imaginative world of goblins and fairy rings.

Life experiences, whether of the everyday or the imagination, impinge on both children and adults, but they impinge differently. For example, politics and disease made death an obvious and likely reality for the Renaissance child and adult alike, but psychological responses to the reality find differing context and expression, depending on age and experience. Fairy stories, known to children and adults, are another example. They were—and are—passed down as part of an oral tradition, a tradition which in medieval and early Renaissance times had belief attached to it. But fairies are eventually appropriated by children and to childhood—and finally to the symbolic meaning of childhood—because they partake of and are most representative of the child's experience. A child is inevitably touched by events and attitudes of the larger society, whether they be political, theological, or cultural, and the child's place in these events and attitudes becomes a part of his or her literature and its appeal. The roots of English children's literature are grounded in the lives of the children as those lives are given expression in the general literature of the time.

In his last essay, Woody writes of John Taylor: "Taylor was at no time a member of the literary establishment, many of whose members scorned his efforts and mocked him. Instead, to support himself, Taylor had to find, often to create, new audiences among the readers of popular literature and among readers not being serviced by writers from the elite or 'literary' culture. His publication record, consequently, maps a series of experiments in all sorts of forms as he sought to

discover what would sell and to whom." Early English children's literature has always been on the outskirts of the
attention of the literary establishment. Woody was among
the first of the literary scholars of the English Renaissance to
challenge that indifference. Because no canon or adequate
criteria for it have been available, Woody's own publication
record in the field of early children's literature—the essays
presented in this volume—"maps a series of experiments in all
sorts of forms," experiments that serve as markers for other
scholars of children's literature. "If I succeed in this task," he
wrote, "my study should call for a re-examination of the
origins of English children's literature and re-direct the attention of teachers and scholars to the early period as an abundant storehouse of lively children's literature rather than a
barren wasteland pockmarked by dreary didactic tracts."
Woody's work in early English children's literature lifts the
foundling off the doorstep, takes it inside the house, and
clothes it in its own richly embroidered garments.

JEANIE WATSON

CHILDREN'S
LITERATURE
of the
ENGLISH
RENAISSANCE

ONE

From Caxton to Comenius: The Origins of Children's Literature

Although the early eighteenth century is regarded as the seedbed of English illustrated books for children, behind such popular picture books of the period as John Bunyan's *Divine Emblems*, John Locke's illustrated *Aesop* for children, and the variety of picture books which poured forth later in the century from John Newbery's shop in Westminster, lies a more or less continuous tradition of illustrated printed books aimed at least partially at youthful readers which goes back to the fifteenth century and the advent of printing in England. The English Renaissance produced all sorts of illustrated works, including broadside ballads, fairy poetry, chapbook romances, and emblem books, which had the capacity to catch the attention of the child reader. Out of this run of illustrated books from the fifteenth to the seventeenth centuries, however, three stand out as key works the Renaissance culture thought especially appropriate to the child reader: William Caxton's *Fables of Aesop* (1483), John Foxe's *Acts and*

Fifteenth-Century Studies 6 (1983): 303-23

Monuments or *Book of Martyrs* (1563), and the *Orbis Pictus* of the Moravian minister John Amos Comenius published in 1657 (with an English translation in 1658 by the schoolmaster Charles Hoole).

Although intended for general audiences, both Caxton's book and Foxe's, two of the most profusely illustrated works of the English Renaissance, had a particular applicability to children, a unique reference which gives importance to these books as landmarks in the history of children's reading. More obviously a children's book, Comenius's *Orbis Pictus*, generally considered the fountainhead of illustrated books written especially for children, seeks through its illustrations to demonstrate the viability of a pedagogical theory. I believe these three works are cardinal texts in the early development of illustrated books for children in England. All were enthusiastically recommended for children's reading by schoolmasters and other adult authority figures, and, taken together, the three suggest a comprehensive range of picture-text coordination and use of iconic and realistic illustrations for young readers. Further, as each author aimed primarily at a different end—to entertain, to move, and to instruct—so their books represent distinct stages in the evolution of early illustrated books for children. Thus through an examination of these three classic illustrated books, I hope to illumine the tradition and suggest the surprising potentialities of picture and text coordination which prepared the ground for the flowering of children's picture books in eighteenth-century England.

Most recent critics seem to agree that William Caxton was something more than the dull-witted journeyman printer of older accounts, selecting for print only those titles assured of showing a profit without regard to their intrinsic worth.[1] Instead, a review of the books from his press suggests that he exercised both intelligence and taste in selecting for publication and translation works of proven worth and interest to the cultured classes who bought his books. His selection of *Aesop's Fables*, ever one of the most universally popular of the classics, may thus seem natural. Yet it provokes several questions: why is the book illustrated? how do text and picture coordinate in Caxton's edition? what was Caxton's target audience and is there evidence that he intended to appeal to youthful readers?

Since Caxton eschewed a preface or other statement of intent in his *Aesop*, the matter of his target audience must be speculative, based on circumstantial evidence. *Aesop* was a favorite text in medieval schools, where the Latin fables had long been used to teach language and rhetoric in combination with sound practical morality.[2] This educational tradition stretches unbroken through the English Renaissance, as pedagogues of the stature of Roger Ascham and Sir Thomas Elyot approved the use of Aesop for schoolboys.[3] Although sixteenth-century English schoolmasters preferred Maartan Van Dorp's continental anthology of the fables, Caxton's edition, continuously available through the eleventh printing in 1658, certainly was eminently suitable to school use.[4] Nor did Caxton, like some subsequent Renaissance editors of Aesop, feel constrained to apologize for the apparent simplicity and childishness of the fables. In fact, Caxton had already demonstrated a strong interest in publishing works intended for children. His edition of the *Book of Curtesye* (1477-78) he describes as a "lytill newe Instruccion" for the small child "to stere and remeve You from vice, and to virtu thou dresse,"[5] and his *Book of the Knight of La Tour-Landry*, published the same year as his *Aesop*, is filled with a father's exemplary stories and precepts for his young daughters on virtuous living. Notable also in the *Book of Curtesye* is

Caxton's comment on the type of material to be given the young:

> Chyldren muste be/ of chyldly governance
> And also they muste entretyde be
> With esy thing/ and not with subtylte[6]

Since Caxton was well aware of the pedagogical tradition that introduced Aesop's *Fables*, an "esy thing" children themselves enjoyed, into the school curriculum, his *Aesop* with its simplified language and vivid woodcuts may be plausibly seen as another attempt on the publisher's part to teach the young sound doctrine. From this perspective, the *Book of Curtesye* offers bare precept, the *Book of the Knight of LaTour-Landry* offers instruction with examples for the parent to supply the child, and Aesop combines precept with parable in a form accessible and attractive to the child himself.

The matter of the illustrations of Caxton's *Aesop* is no less interesting than that of his target audience. Caxton was not particularly fond of woodcut illustrations. They do not appear in his publications before 1481, when both the third edition of his *Cato* and the first edition of *The Mirror of the World* feature a few cuts. It is possible, as E. Gordon Duff argues, that prior to this time in England "there was no wood-engraver competent to undertake the work of illustrating his books."[7] Nevertheless, it is also true that after 1481, even after Caxton acquired access to a stock of continental wood-cuts, fewer than half of his books contain illustrations. Most scholars suggest that the reason Caxton chose to illustrate his *Aesop* and not such other superficially kindred books as his *Reynard the Fox* is that for the *Aesop* he worked from a printed version which contained illustrations suitable for use as models. Caxton employed one master woodcutter, aided by either one or two assistants cutting blocks from his designs, to copy the pictures in his original—Julien Macho's French translation of the famous Heinrich Steinhowell collection, printed by Nicholas Philippe and Marcus Reinhard in Lyons in 1480. These French cuts are in turn based on originals in the Latin text with German translation printed about 1477 by Johann Zainer at Ulm. Perhaps the simple weight of this tradition of illustrated *Aesops* in print impelled Caxton to employ woodcutters for his ambitious undertaking. Certainly the 186 illustrations, far more than in any of his other books, makes of Caxton's *Aesop* a unique departure in English printing.

An interesting though inconclusive note that may bear upon the intended audience of Caxton's book concerns the alterations he instructed his woodcutters to make in copying the French cuts. The two most striking alterations I have found deal with female nudity; on two separate occasions, Caxton had a cut altered in order to chasten it. In his translation of the fabulous life of Aesop by the thirteenth-century Byzantine monk Planudes which prefaces both the Steinhowell and Macho translations, an anecdote is related of Aesop's "discovering" the bare backside of his master's wife as she sleeps. The French woodcut records the entrance of the master and a male friend where they are fronted with the sleeping wife's uncovered posterior, her skirt hiked above her waist for maximum exposure. In Caxton's woodcut, however, her dress covers her private parts to reveal only her lower leg and a small portion of thigh. More radically, in the fourteenth fable of Book II, the fable of the wolf and the idol, the French woodcut illustrates a naked female torso as the object of the wolf's meditation. Caxton, however, substitutes one of the Middle Ages' ubiquitous skulls for the potentially prurient idol in both his woodcut and his translation of the tale. There is little evidence from his other publications that Caxton was

Aesop's master discovers his sleeping wife, in Caxton's illustration
and in the French woodcut (top) on which it was based.

a prude. Why did he feel constrained to alter his text in *Aesop*? Perhaps this unaccustomed primness derives from the publisher's knowledge that, unlike most of his other works, his *Aesop* was a book which would exert a strong appeal to youth.[8]

The coordination of picture and text, the pithy little dramas usually featuring talking animals, and the simplicity of style made of Caxton's *Aesop* a natural book for children.[9] Each fable has its own woodcut, the picture generally standing at or near the beginning of the fable. As Edward Hodnett has observed, this physical placement of the cut on the page invites the reader to "read" the illustration before the text.[10] To the youthful or beginning reader, the utility of this arrangement is obvious. The woodcut provides the major actors and usually the central situation of the fable; forearmed with this knowledge acquired through looking at the picture, the child reader is at a distinct advantage in figuring out unfamiliar words on the page. In following the French originals, Caxton's woodcutters generally paid less attention to background materials, omitting much of this to enlarge and heighten the central figures, people and creatures, who more clearly dominate the picture in Caxton than in his continental models. Whether this circumstance is due to the diminished skill of the English artisans or to a conscious artistic or pedagogic decision to heighten and simplify as an aid to comprehension of the text is unsure. What is clear is that the profuse illustrations of birds and beasts in action, closely tied to a simplified text, resulted in the production in Caxton's *Aesop* of the first popular illustrated book printed in England, a book pressed on and welcomed by generations of English schoolchildren.

Approximately seventy years after the appearance of Caxton's *Aesop*, John Foxe began work on the next book I wish to consider. The first two editions of the work which became the *Book of Martyrs* Foxe wrote and published abroad in Latin. However, for the great *Actes and Monuments of These Latter and Perillous Dayes* . . . of 1563 (to give the work its proper rather than its popular title), he forsook the Latin to which his humanist training inclined him, deciding to write instead in the vulgar tongue for the explicit benefit of "the simple flock of Christ, especially the unlearned sort, so miserably abused."[11] In reaching out to the unlearned, Foxe took aim at the broadest English audience, including all classes and all ages; thus his great book contains various strategies for exerting a mass appeal. In particular, his text demonstrates conclusively that youthful readers were one of his primary targets. His stirring tales are replete with stories of children treated as positive and negative exemplars for the juvenile reader. Like their elders, these youth are divisible into the elect, those godly children who obey and succor their elders following the Christian precepts they have been taught, and their wicked brethren, who scorn the path of righteousness to aid the forces of evil, even in one vivid group of stories informing upon their parents to the persecutors.

Foxe holds up various peer-group examples for his young readers throughout his book, occasionally even exhorting them directly to take the lessons to heart, as with the story of an unfortunate little blasphemer who was stricken speechless and shortly died: "And therefore let all young maids, boys, and young men, take example by this wretched silly wench, not only not to blaspheme the sacred majesty of the omnipotent God their creator, but also not once to take his name in vain, according as they are taught in his commandments."

Preachers, parents, schoolteachers, and others with charge over children quickly saw the efficacy of Foxe's moral tales in pointing little feet down the path of righteousness and, consequently, Foxe's book was regularly pressed upon children. By canon decree of 1571 chained to a stand in all cathedral churches in England and placed in the vestibules of ministers' chambers, the great books were readily available to young children. And the many popular Renaissance abridgments intended for study in the home included some like John Taylor's miniature edition of 1617, a volume less than two inches in length and width, which seem especially designed to appeal to young readers. At any rate, Foxe specifically targeted a young audience, and adults cooperated with the martyrologist by urging the work upon children, encouraging them, in the words of Thomas White's *A Little Book for Little Children* (1674), "When thou canst read, read no Ballads and foolish books, but the *Bible* and the *Plain-mans path way to Heaven*, a very plain holy book for you; get the *Practice of Piety;* Mr. *Baxter's* Call to the Unconverted: *Allens* Allarum to the Unconverted; read the Histories of the Martyrs that died for Christ, and in the *Book of Martyrs.*"[12]

Foxe's method of organizing and presenting his *Book of Martyrs* illustrates the techniques through which he intended to reach an unlearned audience. Foxe eschewed the method of a tract, treatise, or sermon and presented instead a fast-paced narrative punctuated by indelible descriptions of heroic and tragic action. In one of his prefaces, Foxe explains that although many learned works and disputations have rebutted the Roman Catholic position, "But to this, none answereth you better than our martyrs themselves, which in this book do tell you, that in the same which you call heresy, they serve the living God" (1:xiv). The heart of Foxe's book then is narrative and descriptive, the stories of the Protestant martyrs functioning as a vivid and unanswerable Protestant emblem to refute the errors of Rome. Nor are Foxe's descriptions only verbal, powerful though they be; his *Book of Martyrs* is one of the most lavishly illustrated English books of the sixteenth century. Foxe commissioned the woodcuts, perhaps even himself providing original sketches for the craftsmen,[13] coordinated them with his text, and added more to subsequent editions as the popularity of the book occasioned additional printings.

The extensive use of illustrations, more than 160 in the second English edition of 1570, extends the range of appeal of Foxe's book even farther, down to illiterate laborers and housewives and, more significant to us, to the preliterate audience of children from toddlers to apprentices. As Frances Yates has observed, there is nothing haphazard about the subjects selected for illustration in the *Book of Martyrs*.[14] They are the great events, the key themes of the work, Christian martyrdom for the true apostolic faith and virulent antipapalism; this is so far true that the major themes of the book may be accurately grasped by viewing the woodcuts, often grouped in sets in Foxe's book, alone without reference to the text. And these woodcuts—of Tyndale in the flames at the stake calling resolutely for the Lord to open the King of England's eyes or of Emperor Henry IV standing barefoot in the snow with his wife and child outside the pope's palace at Canossa while monks and nuns revel within—these illustrations are designed to elicit visceral emotional appeals independent of age, status, or sophistication.

The woodcut engravings in the *Book of Martyrs* fall into three pretty clearly distinguishable groups, as George Williamson notes in his edition.[15] First, there are the small conventional engravings of martyrs which are scattered throughout the text. The same engravings are used repeatedly for different martyrs without any pretence of being original portraits of individual martyrs (although the names are changed for each). Although this repetition blunts the visceral impact of the pictures, these engravings of martyrs

Bishop Bonner scourges a martyr in one of Foxe's realistic illustrations.

peering heavenward through the flames thus help to universalize the individual martyrs by reminding the reader how the sacrifice of these his countrymen has identified them with all those who have ever died for Christ. The second group is composed of larger, more formal engravings combining realistic with allegorical techniques, such as the engraving of Henry VIII trampling the pope. Finally, the most interesting group is composed of realistic engravings of people and events evidently designed from eye-witness reports. Examples of these realistic engravings include the panoramic scene of the burning of a group of Protestants at Windsor or the famous portrait of Bishop Bonner scouring a young Reformer in his garden while even his henchmen must cover their faces and look away out of pity. Whether or not J.F. Mozley is correct in his supposition that Foxe himself might have created the sketches on which such realistic engravings were based, their accuracy and power are graphically attested to by the report that Bonner himself is said to have complained of the accuracy of his likeness in Foxe's engravings.[16]

The close coordination with the text and the apparent realism of the illustrations go far beyond anything in Caxton; both are innovations in English books aimed, at least partially, at children. While it is true that there is a realistic portrayal of heroes and villains in Foxe, the realism is often only tactical, surface deep, while the larger design of the engravings is symbolic, calculated for maximum emotional effect. Thus the subjects are selected in attitudes, poses, and backgrounds which will elicit a given emotional response. The moment of death, the martyr in the flames or under torture are favorites; descriptions are vivid, with subsidiary characters often stylized into craven persecutors or sympathetic bystanders. Frequently, the central characters are posed allegorically, although the iconography of the illustrations in the *Book of Martyrs* is not subtle and could be grasped with little difficulty by most children. And the engravings, like the text itself, become more sensuous, more moving as Foxe revised and added illustrations for new editions. In the first edition of 1563, for example, the reign of Henry VIII, which inaugurates the English Reformation period, lacks any portrait of the monarch. In the 1570 edition, however, an attractive but relatively static portrait of the king surrounded by his council, a woodcut borrowed from Edward Hall's *Chronicle* of 1548, prefaces the account of his reign which begins volume two. Finally, in the 1583 edition, a new picture begins volume two, an inflammatory engraving of Henry in action, trampling the pope underfoot as his counselors look on in supportive admiration.[17]

In Foxe's book, then, the illustrations function organically to serve the author's twin aims, to instruct the reader in the

Henry IV with his wife and child, barefooted, at Canossa (top) and King John surrendering his crown, from the *Book of Martyrs*.

history and truth of Protestantism and to move him in an instinctive antipathy for Catholicism and its agents and to awe at the incredible suffering and triumph of the heroes of the Reformation. Whereas Caxton had sought to instruct entertainingly, Foxe sought to move by working upon the emotions to elicit admiration or repugnance. Thus, even those pictures ostensibly providing information, illustrating scenes in the text, such as King John's surrender of his crown or the humiliation of the Emperor Henry IV before the pope's palace at Canossa, are laced with inflammatory details of libidinous, leering monks and nuns or of Henry's young son, forced to stand barefoot in the snow awaiting the pope's pleasure. The same end, a visceral emotional response, is achieved by the illustrations of the martyrs, such as the gruesome end of William Gardiner, whose exquisite torture by Portuguese papists in 1552 is the subject of a full-page engraving. The ability of the picture book to indoctrinate children through powerful appeals to their emotions is thus first illustrated by Foxe.[18]

The final illustrated book in our trio of Renaissance classics is the *Orbis Pictus Sensualium*, (*The World of Sensible Things Drawn*), by the Moravian pansophist and educational theorist John Amos Comenius. As in the books of Caxton and Foxe, Comenius's illustrations supplement his text to instruct through the addition of an extra, sensuous pleasure. But unlike his predecessors, Comenius spells out the theory and aim of the picture-text coordination, a relationship much closer than in previous books intended for children. Comenius entices and aids the weak reader with prefatory engravings in a fashion similar to that of Caxton's *Aesop*, but his coordination of picture and text is much tighter than in Caxton or even in Foxe. And in the vividness of his sketches and their combination of realism with symbolic ordering and references, Comenius's book challenges comparison with the best of Foxe.

Comenius envisioned a comprehensive scheme of instruction in all branches of knowledge which would commence at birth and extend to approximately the pupil's twenty-fourth year.[19] In infancy, the child was taught through example, instruction, practice, and discipline primarily by his mother in the home. Formal schooling began at age six in the vernacular school, where the child learned to read his native tongue and expand his horizons through the study of books. At age twelve he was to enter the Latin school for advanced study and, finally, from eighteen to twenty-four, he was ready for higher education, preferably in an academy. Comenius wrote textbooks for the latter three educational levels, beginning with his famous *Janua Linguarum Reserata* (1631) (*The Gate of Tongues Unlocked*), a revolutionary new text for teaching Latin through short, topical sentences of clear reference to the student's world. The *Janua* was not illustrated, although in 1637 Comenius expressed a wish that pictures be included in both the *Janua* and the *Vestibulum* if competent engravers could be found. The basic idea for an illustrated text for the teaching of language in elementary school was suggested to Comenius by Professor Eilhardus Lubinus of the University of Rostock, who edited in 1614 a Greek testament in three languages. In the preface to this work, Lubinus had deplored contemporary methods of language instruction, which relied heavily on rote memorization of cases and grammar rules. Instead, he advocated a simplified text containing pictures with brief sentences attached to them. However, neither Lubinus nor anyone else followed through actually to produce and print such a book until Comenius brought out the *Orbis Pictus* in 1657.

An experienced classroom teacher as well as an educational theorist, Comenius sought demonstrable and replicable results from his texts. Thus, when he learned the *Janua* was too difficult for many beginning students, he wrote and published in 1633 the *Vestibulum Latinae Linguae Rerum (The Porch of the Latin Tongue)*, an even more simplified Latin primer made up of 427 short sentences. Comenius regrets the absence of illustrations in this work, lamenting that he could find no competent artists to do the engravings. Thus, he urges teachers to supply the want of pictures by bringing to class the objects described in the *Vestibulum*, so the pupils could more readily associate word and object. Finally, in 1650-53, he found himself assigned the post of director of the school at rural Saros Patek in Hungary. There, the students lacked the basic literacy necessary for the utilization even of the *Vestibulum*, so Comenius turned once more to the long deferred project of an illustrated language book for children which would teach them Latin through the study of familiar objects and occupations. Again, however, Comenius was stymied by the lack of skilled craftsmen in Saros Patek and the region capable of doing the engravings. Finally, he found an obliging printer, Michael Entner of Nuremberg, who employed skilled artisans able to illustrate the book according to Comenius's instructions and sketches. Published in Germany in 1657, the book was immediately successful.

Orbis Pictus was the fullest, and most successful, concrete illustration of Comenius's educational philosophy. As a philosopher, he subscribed completely to the realist position which insisted all knowledge must arise from sense experiences. Hence the tag from Aristotle on the title page of the *Orbis Pictus: Nihil est in intellectu, quod non prius fuit in sensu* (nothing is in the mind that was not first in the senses). The way to teach then is through a direct appeal to the senses, especially the key sense, that of sight. By yoking concrete pictures with words, abstract linguistic markers, Comenius hoped to reassert the union of words and things and, through repetition, impress them upon the pupil. As an experienced teacher of youth, Comenius buttressed his philosophical beliefs with direct observation of his charges. Children, he noted, are most easily reached through their senses, for, writes Comenius, "it is apparent that Children (even from their Infancy almost) are delighted with Pictures, and willingly please their eyes with these sights."[20] Indeed, the younger the child the stronger the senses, "for the senses (being the main guides of child-hood, because therein the Mind doth not as yet raise up it self to an unobstructed contemplation of things) evermore seek their own objects" (A4); thus through the use of pictures coordinated with text, Comenius's method will ensure that the child "may be furnished with the knowledge of the Prime things that are in the world, by sport, and merry pastime" (A5v). In his preface to the *Orbis Pictus*, Comenius provides a comprehensive and coherent examination of the necessity for illustrated children's books which goes beyond the discussions of Lubinus, Erasmus, and earlier commentators. Here he spells out the heart of his theory:

The ground of this business is that *sensual objects be rightly presented to the senses*, for fear they may not be received. I say, and say it again aloud, that this last is the foundation of all the rest: because *we can neither act nor speak wisely, unlesse we first rightly understand all the things which are to be done, and whereof, we are to speak. Now there is nothing in the understanding which was not before in the sense. And therefore to exercise the senses well about the right perceiving the differences of things, will be to lay the grounds for all wisdom, and all wise discourse, and all discreet actions in one's course of life.* Which, because it is commonly neglected in Schooles, and the things that are to be learned are offered to Scholars, without being understood, or being rightly presented to the senses, it cometh to pass, that the work of teaching and learning goeth heavily onward, and affordeth little benefit. [A3-A4v]

Thus the entertainment provided by the pictures is not an end but only a part of the method; nor is the end even the learning of Latin, which remains, at least to Comenius's mind, only a mediate goal. Instead, through the illustrations of carefully selected and ordered objects and activities, Comenius aimed to furnish the child with nothing less than a fundamental, comprehensive grasp of the universe about him (*Hoc est, omnium fundamentalium in Mundo Rerum, & in vita Actionum, Pictura & Nomenclatura*, boasts the title page). The key to this technique is picture-text coordination. In Caxton's *Aesop*, some of the engravings capture the central incident of the fables but others do not; occasionally, there are only stylized cuts of animals talking or moving in general, non-specific contexts. Similarly, for all of Foxe's realistic woodcuts, the symbolic cuts of a resigned and confident martyr standing amidst the flames, illustrations used over and over in the *Book of Martyrs*, add little to the impact of the text. But for the *Orbis Pictus*, each engraving is fresh, clear, and uncluttered, answering exactly to the single sentences it is designed to illustrate.

Comenius's method keys each significant object in a respective engraving to the sentences, in parallel columns of Latin and vernacular, which follow by numerals inscribed on the engravings and repeated in the text. Thus, object and word are yoked, and visual and verbal stimuli brought into play. In a simple, clear, and entertaining fashion, the correlation between word and thing is established for the beginning reader. The engravings are designed to be as attractive as possible to children's imaginations, even when their interests do not always coincide with the real sensible objects Comenius wished to teach them about. Thus, for example, in a cut

Serpents and creeping things.

entitled "Serpents and Creeping Things," along with snakes
and lizards Comenius includes illustrations of a dragon, "a
winged Serpent [which] killeth with his breath" and the
Basilisk, which kills "with his eyes" (65). Although well aware
that these picturesque relics from medieval bestiaries did not
exist, the clever seventeenth-century schoolmaster knew
that children's interest in them remained strong. And, on the
other side of the page, Comenius also tailored his text to the
students' capacities and interests, explaining to them in a
discussion of the Flesh and the Bowels, for example, that the
"skin being pull'd off ye flesh 2. appeareth, not in a continued
lump, but being distributed, as it were into stufft puddings
which they call muscles" (82).

Although Comenius appealed to the immediate sensory
world of children, this appeal was not his primary purpose.

What he wanted to give young readers was an accurate
understanding of the universe around them. Thus he arranged his picture book in a sequence calculated to do so.
First there is an introductory cut in which the Master invites
the boy to come learn and become wise and a vocal alphabet
of sounds illustrated by cuts of the creatures who utter them.
Comenius then devotes eight chapters to God and the building blocks of His universe, the four elements. The next
thirty-five chapters convey the scholar up the Chain of Being
from the vegetable kingdom to the animal and finally to man,
whose ages, types, and parts are explored in vivid detail.
Next, in the longest section of the book, over one-third of
the text, Comenius describes the various Arts and Sciences
for the child, showing the implements and methods of agri-
culture, beekeeping, baking, fishing, hunting, cooking, and
many other practical occupations. The final quarter of the
text includes chapters on natural and moral philosophy, social life, politics and war, and religion. In the concluding
chapter, which repeats the woodcut of the teacher and pupil
from the introduction, the child is promised that with this
concrete introduction to the real world and the solid grounding in language provided by the text, he is ready to "Go on
now, and read other good *Books* diligently, and thou shalt
become *learned, wise, & Godly*" (309).

In Comenius's book, the full didactic potential of the
picture-book for children is finally realized. Where Caxton's
woodcuts had provided an additional pleasure while functioning as an occasional pedagogical aid and Foxe's vivid
engravings had worked upon the emotions to move the
young reader to terror and awe, Comenius reasserted the
pedagogical function of pictures in the educative process.
The engravings, one on almost every other page, first attract
the child who absorbs their images of human and natural

Cornix cornicatur.   *á á* A a
𝕿𝖍𝖊 𝕮𝖗𝖔𝖜 𝖈𝖗𝖞𝖊𝖙𝖍.

Agnus balat.   *bé é é* B b
𝕿𝖍𝖊 𝕷𝖆𝖒𝖇 𝖇𝖑𝖆𝖙𝖙𝖊𝖙𝖍.

Cicáda ſtridet.   *ci ci* C c
𝕿𝖍𝖊 𝖌𝖗𝖆ſ𝖍𝖔𝖕𝖕𝖊𝖗 𝖈𝖍𝖎𝖗𝖕𝖊𝖙𝖍.

Upupa dicit.   *ду ду* D d
𝕿𝖍𝖊 𝖂𝖍𝖔𝖔𝖕𝖕𝖔𝖔 ſ𝖆𝖎𝖙𝖍.

Infans éjulat.   *é é é* E e
𝕿𝖍𝖊 𝕴𝖓𝖋𝖆𝖓𝖙 𝖈𝖗𝖞𝖊𝖙𝖍.

Ventus flat.   *fi fi* F f
𝕿𝖍𝖊 𝖜𝖎𝖓𝖉 𝖇𝖑𝖔𝖜𝖊𝖙𝖍.

Anſer gingrit   *ga ga* G g
𝕿𝖍𝖊 𝕲𝖔ſ𝖊 𝖌𝖆𝖌𝖌𝖑𝖊𝖙𝖍.

Os halat.   *háh háh* H h
𝕿𝖍𝖊 𝖒𝖔𝖚𝖙𝖍 𝖇𝖗𝖊𝖆𝖐𝖊𝖙𝖍
    𝖔𝖚𝖙.

Mus mintrit.   *í í* I i
𝕾𝖍𝖊 𝕸𝖔𝖚ſ𝖊 𝖈𝖍𝖎𝖗𝖕𝖊𝖙𝖍.

Anas tetrinnit.   *kha kha* K k
𝕿𝖍𝖊 𝕯𝖚𝖈𝖐 𝖖𝖚𝖆𝖈𝖐𝖊𝖙𝖍.

Lupus úlulat.   *lu ulu* L l
𝕿𝖍𝖊 𝖂𝖔𝖑𝖋 𝖍𝖔𝖜𝖑𝖊𝖙𝖍.

Urſus múrmurat.
                          mum mum
𝕿𝖍𝖊 𝕭𝖊𝖆𝖗 𝖌𝖗𝖚𝖒𝖇𝖑𝖊𝖙𝖍.   M m

activity. Then, after the original visual stimulus provided by the child's discovery of the picture, Comenius shows the child how to look again, how to read the picture a new way through the use of numerical tags attached to the principal objects in each woodcut. These are explained sequentially in simple language, first in the vernacular and then in Latin, both languages employing the numerical references to the pictures. Then, Comenius's book moves the child from the spontaneous pleasure of discovery to the disciplined pleasure of the acquisition of knowledge.[21]

These three famous illustrated books of the Renaissance indicate both the span and the evolution of picture books during the period. The origins of the illustrated children's book are firmly planted in the fifteenth century, when the success of Caxton's *Aesop* demonstrated the pedagogical potential of pictures to entertain and assist the apprentice reader's grasp of the text. Foxe utilizes graphic engravings in the *Book of Martyrs* as a potential emotional vehicle for driving home the message of his text, burning the story of the Reformation into the psyches of his youthful readers. Finally Comenius illustrates in *Orbis Pictus* how a coherent pedagogical method, applied systematically, can teach effectively and entertainingly through the minute coordination of picture and text. Thus, it seems just to view these three classic books as clearly demarcating the critical stages in the evolution of illustrated books for youthful readers in England prior to the eighteenth century.

TWO

Childermass Sermons in Late Medieval England

The following discussion is a survey of an abstruse but fascinating subject, the Childermass ceremonies in medieval England and, in particular, the children's sermons preached by boys (and apparently also by girls in some places) on the Feast of the Holy Innocents, December 28, from at least the thirteenth through the sixteenth centuries all across England. Although the festivities of which these sermons were a part have attracted the attention of scholars, chiefly students of drama history seeking early manifestations of the dramatic impulse in ecclesiastical custom and ritual, the sermons themselves have been almost completely neglected. I intend to examine these sermons, assessing their literary and historical importance along with their claim to a place in the literary history of the late Middle Ages in England. But first, the sermons must be put back into their original context, which requires a discussion of how children came to deliver sermons in the first place and, in particular, a consideration of the ceremonies surrounding the festivities of both the Feast of the Holy Innocents and those on St. Nicholas' Day in the medieval and early Renaissance English church.

Fifteenth-Century Studies 4 (1981): 195-205

We first hear of a distinctive celebration involving children on Holy Innocents' Day in a notice from the monastery of St. Gall on the continent in the early tenth century.[1] Here in place of the regular clerical officials, the children are record-ed as processing reverently through the church. This notice is interesting for two reasons. First, it is a reminder that whatever the children's celebrations may have subsequently become, originally they were a serious affair, commemorat-ing Herod's slaughter of the children, martyrs who in a sense were the first to die for Christ and who, in their innocence, prefigured and typified the sacrifice of the Cross. Second, this early notice distinguishes the children's celebrations from the adults' riotous Feast of Fools, which arose some two centuries later and tarred the various Christmas festivities with its notoriety. In fact, the connection occasionally sug-gested of the children's celebrations with the Feast of the Ass held in some medieval churches or with the ancient Roman Saturnalia or Kalends, celebrated in December and featuring a Juvenilis or Youths' Day, is very speculative.[2]

What is sure is that the medieval church included in the Christmastide celebrations three feasts held on three separate days presided over by the different ranks of the clergy. These feasts, called the *tripudia*, were held by the deacons on De-cember 26, St. Stephen's Day, in honor of Stephen the proto-deacon, by the priests on December 27, the feast of St. John the Baptist the proto-priest, and by the choirboys on Holy Innocents' Day, December 28. Subsequently, the sub-dea-cons, an ill-defined order on the fringes of the clergy, set up a feast on Circumcision Day, January 1, which rapidly evolved into the drinking, blasphemy, and riot popularly called the Feast of Fools. Of these various feasts, the Holy Innocents' celebration was both the most popular and the most impor-tant. The feast survived the ecclesiastical suppression during the Middle Ages of the contiguous Feast of Fools and, once the cult of St. Nicholas of Myra was joined to the Holy Innocents' celebration, the feast bequeathed to us Santa Claus, the giving of gifts, and other pleasant Christmas customs. Apparently some time during the late eleventh or early twelfth centuries, the cult of St. Nicholas, the patron of children, thieves, seamen, and especially, for his marvellous rescue of the pickled schoolboys, the patron of students and scholars, was introduced into Western Europe. St. Nicholas's Day, December 6, was not only celebrated by children and students with feasting and plays but soon the custom of electing the boy to preside as Child Bishop on Holy Innocents' Day was moved back to St. Nicholas Eve in early December. Indeed, at Beverly, and perhaps elsewhere in England, the Boy Bishop even officiated at divine services on St. Nicholas's Day just as he did on Holy Innocents' or Childermass Day, as it came to be called. There is no record of children's sermons being preached on St. Nicholas's Day, however.

The earliest notice of the Boy Bishop ceremony in England occurs in a statute at York Cathedral before 1221 specifying some of the youth's duties, and there are additional records of Boy Bishops at Salisbury and St. Paul's Cathedral within the same decade. Although popular throughout Europe, the practice, which was fully sanctioned by the Catholic church, was a particular favorite of the English and spread rapidly throughout the land. It is difficult to tell exactly when the Childermass ceremonies spread from the monasteries and collegiate churches to the ordinary parish churches and schools of England, but the ample surviving records of miniature copes, rings, staffs, and the like for use by the Child Bishops from churches all over England supplement the regulations and notices of the practice to suggest that by the late fifteenth century most English parish churches had their own Boy Bishops.

The Salisbury Processional and Breviary give us our clearest picture of the Childermass ceremonies as practiced in England.[3] In brief, for the twenty-four hours beginning with Vespers on Holy Innocents' Eve, the choir boys or schoolboys (sometimes both) took the place of their elders, assuming their rights, duties, and privileges in the performance of religious services. Their chief was the Boy Bishop (*Episcopus Puerorum*—or Child's Bishop, Barne Bishop, Nicholas Bishop, Innocents Bishop, Scholars Bishop, as he was variously called) elected back on St. Nicholas' Day by his fellows, a prerogative jealously guarded by the boys who successfully resisted, at York and elsewhere, their elders' attempts to abolish the electoral process in favor of a Boy Bishop appointed by the adults. On Childermass Eve the Boy Bishop with his attendants led a procession from the choir either to the altar of St. Nicholas or that of the Holy Innocents, the Holy Trinity, or All Saints in the chapel, where like a real bishop he censed the altar and the image of the saint. He blessed the people and led his procession back to the choir where the boys took the higher stalls and kept them until Vespers on Childermass Day. A sumptuous supper followed. On Childermass Day all the services, with the possible exception of mass, were performed by the Boy Bishop and the boys. Also in the morning, in England at least, it was the custom for the Boy Bishop to deliver a sermon to his fellows, his masters, and townspeople who came to celebrate the feast. A dinner followed, after which the Boy Bishop and his retinue processed through the streets on horseback. This public procession was one of the popular highlights of the ceremonies; indeed, it drew such a crowd that a statute was necessary in 1319 at Salisbury prohibiting people, under pain of excommunication, from pressing on or disturbing the Boy Bishop's procession. The Boy Bishop then accepted gifts and levied contributions, and a variety of entertainment was featured including plays, probably some on the Slaughter of the Holy Innocents and on St. Nicholas' miracles, dancing, and masking. In the evening there was another procession and dinner. The fortunate lad chosen Boy Bishop received all contributions to the church on Holy Innocents' Day, but his privileges extended well beyond the feast day. For better than the next month, until Candlemas, February 2, the Boy Bishop, with his staff and a select company of youthful singers, travelled about the country being feted and receiving contributions from citizens, churches, and institutions in the area. Indeed, from the records at York, the Boy Bishop went to school only one day in the month between Childermass and Candlemas, and on that one day it is noted that he went out of town as soon as he had breakfast.

With its combination of the serious and the festive, the Childermass ceremonies proved continuously popular in medieval England. Indeed, there are records of convents and girls' schools setting up their own Christmas children's feast. A letter survives from the Archbishop of Canterbury in the thirteenth century to the Abbess of Godstow nunnery warning her that they "should not do elsewhere what is done by Holy Virgins on Innocents Day and let the sacred offices and prayers be offered by girls."[4] And as late as 1526, another bishop condemned the election of a child abbess at Carrow Nunnery. While most scholars, such as Karl Young and A.F. Leach, attribute the essential popularity of the feast to the revelry and masking which attended it, the more serious side of the ceremonies, especially in England, must have provided a broadly based bulwark against the sort of official edicts which swept away the Feast of Fools in England. Attempts to curb the festivities are recorded as early as the mid-thirteenth century where, at St. Paul's, regulations were made to curtail the playing and processions because, in the words of the register, "what had been invented for the praise of sucklings had been converted into a disgrace, and to the derision of the decency of the House of God, on account of the unruly crowd which followed it, and the riotous mob which disturbed the Bishop's peace."[5] The effective suppression of the Boy Bishop did not take place until the mid-sixteenth century, when Henry VIII issued a proclamation in 1541 forbidding the practice in Protestant England and levelling far more serious charges at it than the unruly behavior of the spectators. The royal proclamation read in part:

> Whereas heretofore dyvers and many superstitions and chyldysh obseruances have be vsed, and yet to this day are observed and kept, in many and sundry parts of this realm, as vpon Saint Nicholas, Saint Catherine, Saint Clement, the Holy Innocents, and such like, children be strangelie decked and apparayled to counterfeit priestes, bishoppes, and women, and so be ledde with songes and daunces from house to house, blessing the people and gatheryng of money; and boyes do singe masse and preache in the pulpitt, with syche other vnfittinge and inconuenient vsages, rather to the derysyon than any true glory of God, or honor of his sayntes: The Kynges Maiestie therefore, myndinge nothinge so moche as to aduance the true glory of God without vaine superstition, wylleth and commandeth that from henceforth all svch superstitious obseruations be left and clerely extinguished throwout his realmes and dominions, for asmvch as the same doth resemble rather the vnlawfull superstition of gentilitie, than the pure and sincere religion of Christe.[6]

The heart of Henry's charge is that the children made a travesty of the divine service and especially that they blas-

phemed in performing the mass and preaching a mock sermon. But while the dancing and singing festivities outside the
church on the afternoon of Holy Innocents probably became
excessive in places, there is little evidence that the boys'
services were irreverent, and certainly the surviving Boy
Bishops' sermons are serious exhortations, not parodies or
mocks, despite the complaint of later writers, such as the
sturdily Protestant Elizabethan critic George Puttenham,
who in *The Art of English Poesie* accused the Boy Bishops of
"preaching with such childish terms as to make the people
laugh at his foolish counterfeit."[7] As regards the children's
singing the mass, some surviving statutes specifically pro-
hibit it while others imply that the children did perform
every part of the service including the mass. Scholars are
divided on the question, and it need not detain us here. It
suffices to note that Henry managed to suppress the custom
for a time until it was revived under the rule of his Catholic
daughter Mary; it was one of the popular old customs revived
during her reign only to disappear with her passing.

The Childermass celebrations could scarcely have been
less popular with the boys themselves than with the adult
spectators. Medieval schooling seems to have been a rigorous
affair featuring long hours and liberal applications of the rod.
Holidays during the school term were exceedingly rare when
they existed at all; our modern schedule of long holidays,
term breaks, and the like dates only from the eighteenth
century. There were saints' days which were observed in the
monastic schools, but as A.F. Leach has observed, here the
boys simply exchanged a long day in the classroom for a long
day in chapel. But the Childermass celebrations provided a
genuine holiday, a release from the rigors of academic drudg-
ery, a release which, for the fortunate youth chosen as Boy
Bishop and his retinue, could be prolonged through visita-

tions for better than a month. While the festival thus allowed for the venting of youthful exuberance, it also served a psychosocial function. In their solemn mimicry of the religious services, the youths had an opportunity to test themselves in adult roles; perhaps in this connection the ceremonies might even have had a subsidiary effect, in a positive academic sense, giving them a brief taste of the power and prestige to which hard work and close attention to their studies could lead. Certainly for the senior boy who acted the Boy Bishop part the ceremonies must have functioned as a rite of passage symbolizing his own readiness to exchange the world of childhood for that of adult responsibility.

Although the sermons of the Boy Bishops were both popular in nature and serious in intent, especially considering that preaching of any kind was rare in medieval England outside the great cathedrals, few have survived, perhaps because as juvenilia they were not worth preserving or, more likely, not worth printing. At least three were printed, however: an anonymous sermon delivered by the Boy Bishop at St. Paul's printed at least twice, the first time in the final decade of the fifteenth century by Wynkyn de Worde; another sermon by one J. Alcock printed in the fifteenth century by R. Pynson but now lost;[8] and one by the great Dutch humanist Erasmus, apparently written for delivery at his friend John Colet's new boys' school at St. Paul's. Erasmus's sermon, entitled *A Sermon of the Chylde Jesus Made by the Most Famous clerke Doctour Erasmus of Roterdā./ To be pronounced and preached of a chylde unto chyldren*, was printed in an English version by R. Redman probably in the 1540s; a unique copy survives in the British Museum. Also in the British Museum is a manuscript of what may be the last Boy Bishop's sermon preached in England; written by one Richard Ramsey, almoner of Gloucester Cathedral, it was "pronownsyd" by John Stubs, the Boy Bishop in 1558 during the brief period between the death of Queen Mary and the coronation of Elizabeth. The Gloucester sermon was printed for the first time, along with the anonymous St. Paul's sermon, in the nineteenth century by the Camden Society.[9] Thus, although only three Boy Bishops's sermons are presently known to survive, given the length and breadth of the custom's popularity in England, personally I would be surprised if a careful check of the manuscript holdings of church and cathedral libraries in England would not yield more. Certainly in the fourteenth and fifteenth centuries we hear of priests bequeathing collections of copies of Boy Bishops' sermons to their almonries.

Perhaps the most interesting historical question concerning the sermons is that of their authorship. Although all three of the surviving sermons are written from a child's point of view, with apologies for the speaker's juvenile lack of eloquence and frequent asides to his fellows, two of the three are apparently the work of adults. Hence, most scholars assert on this basis that the Boy Bishop sermons were composed by adults, usually one of the almoners like Richard Ramsey at Gloucester Cathedral.[10] But the evidence is far from conclusive. There are frequent references, even in Ramsey's sermon, to the intimate details of the youthful speaker's recent experiences in and out of the choir-loft with his fellow choristers that certainly have the sharp ring of authenticity. As illustrated by the boys at York in the struggle over the selection of the Boy Bishop, the boys guarded jealously the prerogatives of the Childermass ceremony. It seems unlikely that they would willingly give over an opportunity, for example, to rebuke publicly ineffective or overly severe schoolmasters, as the anonymous St. Paul's sermon does in witty fashion. Finally, there is nothing in these extant sermons beyond the wit of a bright youth; they are not larded with citations of the Fathers or references to obscure commentaries. The Boy Bishops were customarily senior boys, whose ages would have varied from thirteen or fourteen at the large collegiate schools to seventeen or eighteen at the monasteries. At this age, they would certainly have been capable of composing an adequate sermon. In the absence of concrete evidence to the contrary, then, the most plausible theory of composition points to a collaboration between the youth who would deliver the sermon and one or more of the masters or almoners.

The three sermons have several emphases in common. First, each is designed from the point of view of a child and consequently each is concerned with the type and level of rhetoric appropriate to the work. Thus in the anonymous St. Paul's sermon the Boy Bishop asks that in "this symple exhortacyon, that I a chylde, wantynge the habyte of connynge, maye be dyrected" (p. 3) by God in his speech. The Gloucester Boy Bishop swiftly resolves the question of rhetorical proficiency, arguing that "Because I kan not speake perfectly and eloquently shall I speake nothing at all? . . . Speake I must, allthough lyke a child, and stammer owt of this word of God a briefe exhortation to both sortes, the elders and yongers, as well as I kan" (p. 20). Erasmus, characteristically, is most sensitive to this aesthetic question, and he has his youthful speaker argue the distinction between a polished worldly eloquence and the straightforward rhetoric of God, affirming that "A chylde goynge aboute to speake before chyldren of the ineffable chylde Jesus wyll not wyshe the eloquence of Tullie/ which myghte stryke the eares with shorte and vayne pleasure/ for how much Chrystes wysdom is dystaunce from the wysdom of the worlde (the dystaunce is unmeasurable) so much ought the christen eloquence dyfferre frō the eloquence of the worlde."[11]

While each sermon aims to set forth the simple Christian rhetoric of youth, in pursuit of that goal each utilizes distinctive stylistic characteristics. The anonymous St. Paul's sermon is direct and homely in its references, teaching primarily through familiar analogies. The Gloucester sermon is racy and colloquial, with a spicy vernacular flavor that leads J.W. Blench to cite it as a premier example of the mid-Tudor colloquial style in his standard study of English Renaissance preaching.[12] Erasmus, whose theories of education transformed the English school curriculum along humanist lines, features prominently in his schoolboy's sermon the techniques he advocated elsewhere for use in teaching rhetoric in the schools, especially the stress on copiousness, the piling up of synonyms until an object or idea has been covered from every angle. Similarly, he uses the basic rhetorical tropes learned early by schoolboys, such as praise by comparison, as in the praise of Christ by comparison which is first considered and then rejected in the sermon due to the incomparable nature of the subject, Christ, whom any comparison must diminish rather than exalt. Both the technique of comparison and the rejection are standard strategies which should have imparted extra pleasure to the boys listening as one of their fellows utilizes the materials of their studies.

There are other common features in these sermons which must have been standard in Childermass sermons. For example, each sermon is careful to expand on the memorial function of the feast, the commemoration of the original slaughter of the innocents by Herod. The audience is reminded not only of the purity and innocence of these little martyrs, but also of their prerogative as the first martyrs for Christ, and also their uniqueness in dying not only for the spirit and faith of Christ but also for his body, giving their lives in place of His. And each sermon rehearses and reexamines the New Testament comments on children, especially the key text of Matthew 18, which the Gloucester sermon takes as its epigraph, Christ's admonition to the apostles that "Except yow will be convertyd, and made lyke unto lytill children, you shall not entre in the kingdom of heaven" (p. 14). The discussions of this and allied Biblical texts raises a central concern of these sermons: their view of the state of childhood.

All of these sermons interpret the Biblical enthusiasm for childhood as the praise of a symbolic cluster of mental and moral attitudes desirable for all men. The Gloucester sermon includes as the body of the text serial addresses to adults in the audience, children, and finally schoolmasters, advising each group on how to capture, retain, and exercise these virtues of what may be called "childship," the state in which we become, as the Gloucester sermon phrases it, "in likeness of manners as young babes, which are simple, without guile, innocent, without harm, and all pure without corruption, as few above the age of childer are" (p. 15). Innocency is the essence of this ideal of childship, for if the prophet warns us to "shun the evill, and do the good," then the innocent are, as Richard Ramsey observes, "halfe the way to the kingdom" (p. 22). All the sermons make clear that one does not achieve this state by a soft relapse into a hazy world of childhood nostalgia; instead, childship is attained only by an effort of will, disengaging oneself from the alluring gins and snares of this world and focusing, with God's aid, on divine love and mercy. This latter is so far necessary that the anonymous St. Paul's sermon asserts that since man is so utterly dependent on God's grace as the infant is on the care of his parents, the child is an apt paradigm of the human condition in this life.

Chronological childhood is not then venerated after the fashion of a subsequent generation of Romantics. All the sermons note that there are certain aspects of childhood such as frivolity, ignorance, and the like which are to be avoided. Nor do all, or even most, children themselves measure up to the ideal of childship. The Gloucester sermon casts about the audience in search of a virtuous child to serve as an exemplar of childship, but the speaker is compelled to reject successively the city children, the school children, and his fellow choristers. As to these latter, the Boy Bishop reflects that

Yt is not so long sens I was one of them myself but I kan remembre what shrewdness was used among them, which I will not speake of now; but I kan not let this passe ontouched how boyyshly thei behave themselves in the church, how rashly thei cum into the quere without any reverence; never knele nor cowntenaunce to say any prayer or Pater noster, but rudely squat down on their tayles, and justle wyth ther felows for a place; a non thei startes me owt of the quere agayne, and in agayne and out agayne, and thus one after an other, I kan not tell how oft nor wherfor, but only to gadd and gas abrode, and so cum in agayne and crosse the quere fro one side to another and never rest, withowt any order, and never serve God nor our Lady with mattyns or with evynsong, no more then thei of the grammer scoles; whose behaviour is in the temple as it were in ther scole ther master beyng absent, and not in the church God being present. I will not wysh you to folow such. [pp. 24-25]

Other sermons also speak of the various punishments, from tweaking of ears and raps on the knuckles through beatings with the rod, necessary to curb unruly youth. The Gloucester sermon, in a refrain familiar to many moderns, places the primary blame for childish corruption upon permissive parents who coddle their children when firmness is wanted instead. Indeed, only Erasmus, caught up for a moment in rhapsodizing childhood, approaches even briefly the neo-Platonic exaltation of the child as repository of secret divine wisdom. "There is universally in the very age of childre," he writes, "a certayne natyve and naturall goodnes/ and as it were a certayne shadowe and ymage of innocencye or a hope rather and dysposition of a goodnes to come. A softe minde and plyable to every behavour/ shamefastnes which is a good kepar of innocencie/ a wytte voyde of vyces/ bryghtnes of bodye/ and as it were a flower of a floryshyng worlde/ and (I can not tell how) a certayne thynge alye and familiare to spirites. For it is not for naught that as ofte as the aungels appeare with thy shewe themselfes in chylderns lykenes" (Bv).

In addition to the features they share, each of these sermons has distinctive strengths which illustrate avenues of development within the tradition of the Childermass sermon. The anonymous St. Paul's sermon is notable for a humorous attack upon schoolmasters who favor the rod. With appropriate classical allusions and pedagogical periphrasis, the young scholar heartily wishes for the speedy promotion of his masters "to be perpetuall felowes and collegeners of that famouse college of the Kynges foundacyon in Southwerke that men call the Kynges Benche [one of the principal London gaols]. . . . And . . . I wolde they shoulde ende ther lyf in that holy way . . . called in Latin *Via Tiburtina*: in Englysshe asmoche to saye as the highe waye to Tyburne" (where thieves and highwaymen were hanged) (p. 4). This levity gives way in the center of the sermon, however, to a fascinating analysis of childhood and childship. The speaker distinguishes three ages of man, each with its own rules and dispensations. The infant, from birth to six, lives under the Law of Kind, free of constraints and responsibility, leading an amoral, natural existence. Then as a youth, or *juventus*, he is sent to school to learn his lessons and mend his morals with close supervision and sure punishment

for lapses. Here he lives under the Law Written, analogous to
the strict Old Testament commandments. Finally, at puberty
in his early to mid-teens, he emerges into adulthood, where
he inherits the Law of Grace, the possibility of salvation
through God's mercy and Christ's sacrifice. The St. Paul's
sermon analyzes these stages, applying them to the history
of the race, for example, as well as to contemporary every-
man. This sermon, the speaker further explains, is especially
aimed at those youths attempting the difficult transition to
adulthood, those "in specyall from xiiij. yeres unto xviij., in
the whiche he is ful of undevocyon, and all moost forgetith to
worshyp his God or ony saynt. And yf he do it with his
mouthe, his herte is ful ferre from God aboute worldly
vanytees" (p. 10).

The body of the Gloucester sermon by Richard Ramsey,
the most formally structured of the three, is composed of the
seriatim addresses to the elders, the children (both "boys and
wenches" according to the text), and to schoolmasters, explaining to each what the ideal of childship should mean to
their stations and lives. This sermon is also interesting as a
Counter-Reformation document. The theme of childship is
popular among English Catholic writers of the mid-Tudor
period, a useful metaphor for arguing that Englishmen should
return to Mother Church like strayed children, loving and
obeying her ways like those of a parent. Certainly the
Gloucester sermon is the most typical of the three, digress-
ing to take a swipe at the Marian Protestant martyrs who are
found to be only pseudomartyrs when compared to the
spotless purity of the Holy Innocents or to notice "how many
witless childer and chyldysh people were in thys realme of
late years and yet are in many places, which waveryd in their
faith" (p. 21).

Finally, Erasmus' sermon focuses on an analysis of Christ's

childhood as a perfect example for both children and adults to emulate. In Christ, argues Erasmus,

Do ye not manifestly see a newe kynde of chyldehood. Of the chyldren in times paste it was sayd. *Stulticia collegata est in corde peuri.* That is to saye. Foly is teyed to gether in a chyldes herte. Of the newe chylde ye here. *Plenus sapientia* full of wysdom/ why do we any longer excuse our rudeness under the cloke of our tender age/ when we heare a chylde not onely wyfe but full of wysdom? Se howe this chylde hathe inverted all order of thynges which sayth in the Apocalyps *Ecce ego nova facio omnia* that is to saye. Lo I make all newe. The wysdom of the aged is destroyed, and the prudence of the prudent is dysalowed/ and chyldren be replenyshed with wysdom. [B9v-B9]

I hope this brief introduction to the Childermass sermons will stimulate further study of this unduly neglected area of medieval literature. For whether or not my suggestions about the authorship of Childermass sermons be accepted, these sermons are virtually unique in the period as imaginative constructs written for delivery by a child to an audience of children and adults with the aim of giving pleasurable instruction in Christian morality. Although they each employ different strategies and techniques to transmit the idea of childship, all three sermons successfully achieve their goal.

THREE

Childhood and Death: A Reading of John Skelton's *Phillip Sparrow*

John Skelton (1450?-1529) wrote prolifically during the final years of the fifteenth and the early years of the sixteenth centuries—in that vague interregnum designated as either late medieval or early Renaissance. Among his poetic productions is *Phillip Sparrow* (written ca. 1508). Coleridge judged it "exquisite and original,"[1] and the poem, rightly so, has always attracted popular favor and critical attention. Yet literary critics have never fit *Phillip Sparrow* comfortably into any generic category. Usually scholars consider it a curious specimen of the mock-elegy, and critics have traced its component parts back to medieval and classical antecedents.[2] Some years ago, however, C.S. Lewis called it "our first great poem about childhood" and suggested that perhaps we were looking at the poem the wrong way.[3] Despite this insight from a noted scholar of both children's literature and sixteenth century poetry, critics have not pursued the suggestion. This essay intends to test Lewis's judgment by

The Journal of Psychohistory 7 (1980): 403-14

investigating *Phillip Sparrow* as a serious poem about child-hood and a poem designed to appeal, on at least one level, to the juvenile reader.

While he wrote the poem, Skelton was residing at Diss in East Anglia, where he held the living of the parish. A classical scholar of recognized ability, Skelton had come late to the ministry, taking orders in his late thirties. He was ordained sub-deacon, deacon, and priest in rapid succession, appar-ently, as his modern biographers speculate, to qualify him for a court position as a suitable tutor to the royal princes, first Arthur and then the future Henry VIII. On the death of Prince Arthur in 1502, Skelton was relieved of his tutorial duties and in 1504 he retired from the court to the living at Diss, where he became acquainted with the leading families of the district, including the Scropes. Jane Scrope, the young girl for whom *Phillip Sparrow* was written, was the daughter of Sir Richard Scrope, an old family friend of Skelton's. She is cast by the poet as the speaker of the first part of the poem.

The striking realism of Skelton's presentation of the wounded psyche of the grieving girl in the poem has always captivated readers. The meticulous detail and empathetic projection manifest in her portrait would suggest similar object losses in the poet's life. While factually this proposi-tion is impossible of proof, since we know nothing of Skel-ton's early life, his parents, or even the year of his birth, psychologically it is as sure as the words on the page. The specific details of his relationship with Jane Scrope are also hazy, although H.L.R. Edwards has reconstructed the back-ground of Jane's arrival at Carrow Priory and speculates upon Skelton's connection with her family.[4] Although the evidence is missing to establish whether Skelton ever functioned as Jane's tutor, his court position with the young princes would have recently reacquainted him with the cries of early adoles-cence.

Jane Scrope had come to the nunnery at Carrow by a painful path. The daughter of a Yorkshire nobleman who died in 1485, an infant no more than a year or two old, Jane grew up in a household headed by her mother and stepfather, Sir John Wyndham. In the violent years following the Tudor capture of the crown on Bosworth Field, as Henry VII consolidated power by removing enemies, Sir John ran afoul of the new regime. In 1501 he was arrested for suspicion of complicity in the Suffolk conspiracy and the following year he was beheaded for treason.[5] The same year, Lady Wyndham removed with her daughters to the Benedictine Priory at Carrow for refuge. Three years later, Lady Wyndham's death left Jane an orphan in the care of the nuns. Although Skelton's poem cannot be precisely dated, most critics regard it as the product of 1506-08; one even raises the intriguing possibility that the funeral being commemorated by the interwoven Latin dirge might be that of Jane's mother.[6] However this may be (and the poem itself offers no clues as to the identity of the deceased), the dedicatee and namesake of the speaker in Part I of the poem was a girl who, in losing not one or two but *three* parents, suffered the reverse of the typical experience of the Renaissance family. Usually, it was the parents who lost, and indeed often expected to lose, children to the myriad mortal dangers that beset childhood in that era.[7] Jane, then, was a physical survivor, and Skelton explores the mental and emotional processes that made possible her psychic survival in the face of traumatic events.

Skelton's poem is veiled. It does not lament the loss of a parent but the death of a pet, a miniature domestic tragedy. As a result of the poet's empathy with the child's grief, the reader is invariably moved to admire and too often to sentimentalize the child in the poem. Noting Jane's sensitivity, her dismay at the death of her bird, a modern reader might imagine how such a child would likely be destroyed by the death of a *person* close to her. Yet from the biographical context external to the poem, we know Jane Scrope had survived parental loss, and the psychological characteristics of the child as survivor are a primary center of interest in the poem. Skelton closely examines her evolving reaction to her pet's death, exploring the psychic mechanism by which a sensitive child withstands and finally conquers the cruelty of death.

Our knowledge of early modern parenting provides several clues to the psychological context of the poem. We know, for example, that parents and children of noble rank in England saw a good deal less of each other in the late medieval and early Renaissance period than at any subsequent time. A child of Jane's rank and status would have been put out of the home for extended periods, from wet-nursing shortly after birth through the customary period of service at the homes of nobility. At that time high infant and child mortality rates, approaching at times 80 percent, militated against parents making major emotional investments in children who likely would not live to see adulthood. Jane's attachment to her pet was very possibly the strongest bond in the orphan's life. Indeed, what is *not* in Skelton's poem may be significant; in attempting to cope with her grief, nowhere does the child think to turn to an adult—neither to Dame Margery or another of the nuns nor to a tutor or a spiritual advisor for guidance and reassurance. Rather, she works through her grief in a psychic isolation punctuated by the ritual of the adult world, the Latin Mass for the Dead being intoned as a backdrop to her personal struggle.[8] The mass is a prefabricated adult formula for dealing with grief; but the object losses the girl in the poem has suffered have made her both independent and skeptical and she does not hasten to attune her "inner weather" to that of adult society. As Lloyd deMause has pointed out in discussing the ambivalent mode

of Renaissance parenting, early modern parents and authority figures sought especially to shape and mold children to
conform to their own notions and projections.[9] Perhaps
because of a tragic personal history which lies largely outside
the details of the poem, the speaker of Skelton's lament has
grown sturdy and independent. She responds by testing and
weighing the adult formulae. Skelton traces the psychic
journey of an extraordinary child in accommodating the grief
of loss.

The original poem of over 1200 lines is structured in two
parts, the first a monologic lament by the girl on the occasion
of the death of her pet bird (the "Lamentations"), the second
an encomium by the poet, not of the dead sparrow, but of the
living girl (the "Commendacions"). In the beginning, Skelton
masterfully creates the persona of the grieving child who
speaks the poem. It was long believed, as Alexander Dyce,
editor of the standard edition of Skelton repeated, that Jane
Scrope was a little schoolgirl when Skelton wrote *Philip
Sparrow* to help console her in her loss. H.L.R. Edwards has
proved, however, that the real Jane was probably in her early
twenties when the poem was composed.[10] Although some
critics argued that this discovery "essentially changes our
view" of the poem,[11] such a radical reevaluation seems both
unnecessary and unwise. Not only can one wonder at the
degree of sophistication or worldliness a day-boarder in a
small Benedictine convent might likely possess, but within
the poem, as both C.S. Lewis and Stanley Fish stress, the
fictional persona of Jane Scrope is imagined as a child, a
schoolgirl with a childlike perspective.[12] In the associational
movement and the peculiar psychic defenses exhibited in the
poem, the psyche of the speaker seems clearly pre-adult.

Despite the hyperbole and local humor of individual lines,
the persona of the grieving girl is neither mocked nor depre-

cated; for the speaker of the poem's first movement, the pain of loss is raw and real. In an attitude sympathetic though not condescending, the poet enters into and limns, in language appropriate to a schoolgirl, the psychic tumult of the child's mind. Through the device of the interior monologue, which is aptly described by one critic as "an early example of the stream-of-consciousness technique"[13] (one of the many paradoxes of this paradoxical poem is its astonishing combination of classical, medieval, and modern techniques and formulas), Skelton explores the girl's sense of loss and traces her various attempts to deal with this unfamiliar emotion. In tracing the girl's successive attempts to come to terms with her loss, Skelton's fidelity to the truths of childhood experience is no less impressive than moving. As an anchor for this exploration of grief, Skelton organizes the poem around three assumptions about the girl's character: she is a practicing Catholic, a well-educated schoolgirl, and a fully sentient child.

While the reader, like the poet of the second, "Commendacions," part of the poem, possesses an emotional detachment and a wider experiential perspective than the child in the poem, Skelton presents her to be taken seriously. Imaginatively and conceptually, the poem explores one of the universal cruces of childhood, the child's first confrontation with the absolute finality of death—and this crux provides the basic ground and structure of the poem. Thus within the first, "Lamentations," section of the poem, the child's confused search for the security of a healing ritual is neither undercut nor patronized. Her quest turns first to religion (lines from the Latin funeral mass recur through this macaronic poem), and then to literature and myth (especially the promise of immortality explicit in classical memorials and literature).

The delicacy, sensitivity, and empathy with which Skelton traces his persona's struggle with grief compose perhaps the most remarkable feature of this most remarkable poem. The poem begins with snatches from the Office of the Dead:

> *Pla ce bo,*
> Who is there, who?
> *Di le xi,*
> Dame Margery;
> Fa, re my, my,
> Wherfore and why, why?
> For the sowle of Philip Sparowe,
> That was late slayn at Carowe,
> Among the Nones Blake,
> For that swete soules sake,
> And for all sparowes soules,
> Set in our bederolles,
> *Pater noster qui,*
> With an *Ave Mari,*
> And with the corner of a Crede,
> The more shalbe your mede.[14]

At the death of her pet, the child's first reflex is to turn to the familiar, soothing phrases from the Psalms for consolation. From her perspective it is neither blasphemous nor irregular to invoke the solemn service for the death of a mere creature. The chief mourner at this service, Jane is aware that her role should be that of a distraught mourner, and she attempts to fit her actions to her conception of that role. She knows the correct signs and symbols of intense grief.

Our knowledge of Jane's parental losses lies outside the conceptual context of the poem. Within the poem, the child seems never to have had to play the role of mourner before. Thus, as Skelton presents the dramatic situation, the bird's murder precipitates in the girl an identity crisis in which her personal resources are tested to the fullest. Here the child struggles to accept and accommodate the finality of death. According to Erik Erikson, in such a crisis the youth "must forge for himself some central perspective and direction, some working unity, out of the effective remnants of this childhood and the hopes of his anticipated adulthood."[15] For Jane, this process is compounded of the familiar elements of the need for devotion coupled with a repudiation of pat adult formulae. Thus, she clings to her religion while reformulating its elements to fit the circumstance of her loss and grief. First, however, she attempts to play the role of mourner as she apprehends it in adult behavior. Jane strikes a series of poses, none the less sincere for their childish exaggeration, and describes them to the reader in theatrical terms as though standing apart to view her own performance. Thus:

> I wept and I wayled,
> The tearys downe hayled;
> But nothynge it avayled
> To call Phylyp agayne
> > [22-26]

> Wherewith my handes I wrange,
> That my senaws cracked,
> As though I had ben racked,
> So payned and so strayned,
> That no lyfe wellnye remayned.
> > [44-49]

> Such paynes dyd me frete,
> That myne hert dyd bete,
> My vysage pale and dead,
> Wanne, and blewe as lead;
> The panges of hateful death

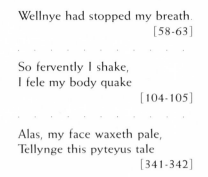

> Wellnye had stopped my breath.
> [58-63]
>
> . . . .
>
> So fervently I shake,
> I fele my body quake
> [104-105]
>
> . . . .
>
> Alas, my face waxeth pale,
> Tellynge this pyteyus tale
> [341-342]

Here Skelton has the child self-consciously and dramatically attempt to pour her pain into the vessels of adult tradition. Her bird deserves no less.

Parallel to these charmingly awkward attempts to attune her grief to the proper key which society and her own reading of epic tragedies have instilled in her, Jane attempts to channel her fresh personal grief into preexistent rhetorical formulas. She hopes to merge her sorrow into a larger social ritual and thereby to distance the loss and dull the pain. She first compares herself to great sufferers of antiquity, but rapidly and wisely abandons this strategy as ill suited to the consolation she seeks. Instead, she turns to the verbal formulas of Christianity, the Latin tags from the Service for the Dead that run only half consciously through her mind along with other varieties of scriptural and religious paraphrase. In the following lines, for example, Jane echoes the familiar *Planctus Mariae* in dramatizing her anguish:

> I syghed and I sobbed,
> For that I was robbed
> Of my sparowes lyfe.
> O mayden, wydow, and wyfe,
> Of what estate ye be,

Of hye or lowe degre,
Great sorowe than ye myght se,
And lerne to wepe at me!
[50-57]

The Christian formulas share place, however, with the classical. For example, Jane chants in the manner of a charm a catalog of classical horrors from which she would have Phillip delivered: great Pluto, foul Alecto, Medusa, Megera, Cerberus, and "the smokes sowre / Of Proserpinas bowre" (82-83). These traditional formulas, Christian and classical, are brought to a climax in an extraordinary prayer which faces both Mt. Olympus and Heaven:

To Jupyter pray we
That Phyllyp preserved may be!
Amen, say ye with me!
    Do mi nus
Helpe nowe, swete Jesus!
[92-96]

In the mind of the child, anxious for the fate of the immortal soul she instinctively imputes to her pet, the traditional formulas of grief and consolation learned from her textbook readings in the classics and the lessons of her catechism flow together and coexist. But neither is sufficient, alone or in conjunction, to mitigate the fresh pain of personal loss. The lovingly detailed portrait of Phillip Sparrow which succeeds the prayer to Jupiter and Jesus in its sharp, sensory detail clearly signals the failure of verbal formulas, Christian or classical, to assuage the child's pain. Instead, the mind recalls a vivid picture of Phillip in a number of familiar domestic poses, sitting on a stool, wearing a tiny velvet cap, chasing grasshoppers, or snuggling his mistress.

With the failure of these rhetorical formulas to provide

relief, Jane turns to survey the prospects for surcease to be derived from physical memorials. She briefly considers the possibility of literary immortality, thinking of the classical poetess's praise of sparrows, but Jane rejects these as unworthy for her Phillip. As her mind returns to the individuality of Phillip, she momentarily indulges in a mental fantasy that perhaps Phillip could be revived and restored to life. After a capsule survey of classical precedents for the miraculous recovery and resurrection of the dead, Jane recognizes the futility of this wish in reflecting upon her own attempt at a physical memorial for Phillip. Once, she relates, she set out to stitch his figure on a sampler that "it myght importe / Some pleasure and comforte / For my solas and sporte" (216-218):

> But whan I was sowing his beke,
> Methought, my sparrow did speke,
> And opened his prety byll,
> Saynge, Mayd, ye are in wyll
> Agayne me for to kyll,
> Ye prycke me in the head!
> With that my nedle waxed red,
> Methought, of Phyllyps blode;
> Myne hear ryght upstode,
> And was in suche a fray,
> My speche was taken away.
> [219-229]

As if in recognition of the psychic toll her grief is exacting, Jane turns from grappling with schemes of consolation which have ended only in hallucination to the simplicity of direct prayer:

> The best now that I maye
> Is for his soule to pray:
> *A porta inferi,*

> Good Lorde, have mercy
> Upon my sparowes soule,
> Wryten in my bederoule!
>   [237-242]

Her prayer begins well enough, a supplication for the intervention of the patriarchs on behalf of her sparrow, whom
they may know by his superiority to all other sparrows. This,
of course, is a reminder to her of the uniqueness of Phillip, a
reminder which abruptly reverses the tone of the poem from
humility to shrill vengeance. For Jane sets out upon an epic
excoriation of Phillip's murderer, that "cat of carlyshe kynde"
(282), Gib the convent mouser. After a seventy-five line
anathema, which encompasses not only Gib but all "vylanous
false cattes" (338), Jane returns to a series of sharp, pictorial
vignettes of Phillip sitting on her finger, drinking her spittle,
and kissing her lips with his beak. Again the fresh pain of her
loss stoked by the vivid recollections called up in her memory effectively blocks any scheme of consolation. A brief
consideration of the fickleness of Fortuna then brings the
poem back to the framing service of the dead with a repetition of its opening lines:

> *Kyrie, eleison!*
> For Phylyp Sparowes soule,
> Set in our bederolle,
> Let us now whysper
> A *Pater noster.*
>   [381-385]

Thus the poem returns, after 385 lines, to its starting
point. The progression in the poem has not been linear, but
vertical, plumbing the depths of the child's sorrow as she
seeks a source of consolation. Skelton has created a map of
childhood grief in the portrait of a mind surveying the

conventional formulas and creeds, secular and Christian, with which the adult world copes with the finality of death. They have not worked for the speaker of Skelton's poem; but this remarkable child is not through yet. For out of the schemes and elements her mind has explored, Skelton's Jane forges a curious individual synthesis in her mind: a Bird Mass combining elements of Christian ritual, classical apotheosis, and native folklore tradition. It comes to her suddenly, almost as the answer to the prayer of helpless supplication which immediately precedes it. Even the excoriation of the treacherous Gib may be seen as a contributing factor to this ultimate *consolatio* synthesis. The pressure of emotion which repeatedly propelled the sharp mental images of Phillip back into Jane's consciousness, defeating the earlier schemes of consolation, is here deflected and momentarily siphoned off upon Gib and all his tribe. The excoriation then functions for the child as a release from emotional bondage, a purgative burning off of strong emotion prior to the reestablishment of temperamental equilibrium and the satisfactory resolution of grief.

In Jane's version of the Bird Mass, seventy-seven birds appear to play their appointed parts in the obsequies for Phillip Sparrow. Quickly the girl becomes immersed in suiting the parts each must play to the physical, moral, or symbolic characteristics of the birds. The ceremony moves to a conclusion again featuring paired prayers, one Christian, the other classical:

> I pray God, Phillip to heven may fly!
> *Domine, exaudi orationem meam!*
> To heven he shall, from heven he cam!
>   *Do mi nus vo bis cum!*
> Of all good praiers God send him sum!

. . . .

On Phillips soule have pyte!
                    [579-583, 586]

. . . .

To Jupyter I call,
Of heven emperyall
That Phyllyp may fly
Above the starry sky,
To treade the prety wren,
That is our Ladyes hen:
Amen, amen, amen!
                    [596-602]

The equilibrium of these twin prayers represents the girl's successful and unique acceptance of her pet's death and her farewell to him, body and soul—his soul commended to empyrean bliss, his body to an eternity of merry copulation. In the fusion of these disparate elements in the medieval Bird Mass at the center of the poem, the classical and Christian archetypes are both supplanted and synthesized, finally assuaging the sense of loss through the fantasy of the avian ceremony. The first movement of the poem, then, concludes with the girl's search for a proper epitaph for the sparrow, which provides a springboard to her discussion of her reading and education. This section of the poem is not, as some have suggested, necessarily proof of Jane's inability to sustain grief, but rather evidence that the correct correlative was discovered, or forged, in the Bird Mass synthesis. It is precisely because the burden of her grief has found an adequate outlet that the child's mind can roam through a mental inventory of her reading in search of a proper epitaph, "in Latyne playne and lyght" (823), for Phillip.[16]

The second movement of the poem, the "Commendacions," finds the poet rather than the child as speaker. Here he praises Jane, not the bird, but in the same rhetorical mode that Jane had employed in fondly recalling her pet—sharp, sensuous, and fully sentient, stressing the beauty of the moment. Indeed, this portion of the poem is almost a *carpe diem* in its celebration of transitory beauty, for the focus is not on the mind but on the physical charms of the girl:

> Soft, and make no dyn,
> For now I wyll begyn
> To heve in remembraunce
> Her goodly dalyaunce,
> And her goodly pastaunce:
> So sad and so demure,
> Behavynge her so sure,
> With wordes of pleasure
> She wold make to the lure
> And any man convert
> To gyve her his hole hert.
> [1093-1102]

While echoing the liturgical framework with snatches of antiphons and verses from the *Commendatio Animae* of the burial service, the poet celebrates the transitory perfection and beauty of youth and the vitality of life in the midst of death. As H.L.R. Edwards has observed, "mysteriously, the elegy becomes transmuted into its opposite—a paean to life, its inexplicable and absurd loveliness."[17] Thus this concluding celebration affords a synthesis that both complements and extends the resolution formulated earlier by the child, imparting to the poem an intellectual and emotional unity often denied it.

In conclusion, then, for an adult *Phillip Sparrow* presents a sensitive exploration of a child's encounter with death, focusing on the metaphysical and emotional confusion and indirection. This ultimately culminates in the healing ritual of the

Bird Mass, a ceremony composed of disparate elements from the different realms of the child's experience. This search for surcease, however, is narrated consistently in the first part of the poem from the point of view of the persona of the child, with the rhetorical simplicity and limited vocabulary proper to the speaker. Skelton's use of an associationist technique as an imitative mode to capture the method and intensity of childhood grief is the most extraordinary technical feature of the poem. From the content of the poem, it is not possible to ascertain whether the dead bird is a substitute love object representing the child's parents, a vehicle for channeling the love her parents were too busy or reluctant to accept and return, or a primary love object, under the care and control of the orphan girl. Whatever the case, however, a knowledge of the historical background of Jane Scrope and the modes of parenting in the early Renaissance enrich a reading of Skelton's poem and authenticate it as a key imaginative record in the development and understanding of childhood in early modern times.

FOUR

The Topos of Childhood in Marian England

The sixteenth century witnessed a renewed interest in child-hood, in the child as creature and symbol, at least as strong in England as on the continent. This interest arose from a number of diverse factors—pedagogical, theological, social, and even political—which I will briefly canvass.

In the area of pedagogy the humanists, inspired by the educational theories of More, Erasmus, and Vives and the example of such innovative new schools as John Colet's at St. Paul's, stimulated interest in discussions of the capacity of a child's intellect and the most effective means of reaching and forming both his mind and character. In addition, all the Tudor monarchs believed in and supported the cause of education, and their patronage is another factor in the new interest in childhood education in England. The rise of public education during the sixteenth century was accompanied and supported by books on educational theory by such English humanists as Elyot, Wilson, Ascham, Mulcaster, and others. During this century, the late medieval custom of removing the child from the home when he had

Journal of Medieval and Renaissance Studies 12 (Fall 1982): 179-94. Copyright © Duke University Press.

attained the capacity for rational thought, usually around seven years of age, for dispatch either to a lengthy apprenticeship to learn a trade or, if of gentle birth, to serve as a page or maid in another's house began to be replaced, or at least preceded by, a period of formal schooling in the grammar schools established by the Tudor government all over England.[1] These schools, set up specifically for the purpose of training children, encouraged a focus on childhood as a specific period of life, as something more than just a time of apprenticeship when the youth strove to grow as rapidly as possible into a trade and take his place in the ranks of responsible and productive citizens.

In sixteenth-century religious controversy, the concept of childhood was one of the many points of contention between conflicting factions. Religious discussions of childhood usually differed from pedagogical ones in that the child was primarily viewed by controversialists in symbolic terms, especially in Catholic writings. In English recusant literature, for example, the child figure became a symbol representing the attitude the English people should take toward the Catholic Church. There seems a fairly consistent separation between real children, the objects of the educational reformers' attention, and the more abstract idea of childhood. Thus, almost all religious factions condoned, indeed encouraged, corporal punishment and other curbs to bring the unruly child into line, while at the same time employing childhood and children as symbolic representatives of a state of innocence, purity, and obedience. The example of childhood is thus a particularly striking instance of the disjunction between symbol and object in sixteenth-century controversy.

The theological controversy had its root in the very different views of childhood espoused by the Catholic Church and the Reformers. The dispute centered on the degree of innocence imputed to children. The Reformers leaned toward the opinion of John Calvin, who wrote "we know that in children many things are corrupt."[2] Children are by nature depraved by original sin; they are "accursed in the wombe," he explained elsewhere: "The very infants themselves, while they bring with them their owne damnation from their mothers wombe, are bound, not by anothers, but by their owne fault. For although they have not as yet brought foorth the fruits of their owne iniquitie, yet they have the seede thereof enclosed within them: yea, their whole nature is a certain seede of sinne: therefore it cannot be but hatefull and abominable to God."[3]

In the face of this stress on infantile original sin, the anti-Calvinists reemphasized and indeed exaggerated the doctrine of original innocence, even to the official adoption by the Council of Trent of a position on the matter which one recent scholar describes as "semi-Pelagian."[4] Certainly the view of childhood innocence held by the two camps was sufficiently different that it could serve as a distinguishing feature. Thus the Catholic position, strongly reiterated and given impetus by the Counter Reformation, is reflected in the ecclesiastical art of the Baroque period which, as Philippe Aries has illustrated, features a surge in the popularity of themes featuring children, most especially Christ's blessing of the children.[5]

There was, of course, a good deal more to the Counter Reformation emphasis on the innocency of childhood than the fact that it represented a clear difference between the religious factions. The potential for childhood innocency, and the cluster of allied virtues—trust, humility, obedience—which usually accompany Catholic discussion of it, as a symbol for a distinctive religious conviction made the topos both a popular and potent one in mid-sixteenth-century Catholic thought and art. To the defenders of Catholicism, reformers had too often abandoned their faith in the verities of the Church to follow their contentious intellects down the road to heresy. On surveying the situation in England upon his return from Italy, Cardinal Reginald Pole, the papal legate to Marian England, complained that every Englishman seemed to have become his own judge in matters divine, each "a studier of Scripture to learne it of his owne wytt and labour," with the lamentable but predictable result that each, having found or formulated for himself a creed, set out to proselytize, Pole relates, "as experience showeth the multitude of teachers and preachers att this a late tymes past."[6] The unfettered pursuit of religious truth through reason, lacking the discipline, guidance, and tradition of the Church, was both a root of heresy and a primary channel for its dissemination, as the new truth of the Reformers had to be argued out through sermons, tracts, and the like. In brief, men had to be persuaded of the reformed position; however, traditional Catholicism, the faith of their fathers, required only loyalty and fidelity. Not unnaturally, Catholic spokesmen put a premium on such virtues and the symbols through which they might be embodied grew correspondingly popular in the literature produced under their aegis.

Cardinal Pole, to return to our example, in his vernacular homilies directed at all Englishmen frequently employs the topos of childhood as symbol of the attitude English Christians should adopt. While individual Scripture study by laymen is not condemned, it is always the interpretation placed on the Scriptures by their father the Pope and mother the Church which should guide Englishmen. "You should not," the cardinal warns his audience, "be your owne masters, whiche were as much to make yourselffes father and mother to your self. But as you take the booke of your mothers hand so also to take the interpretatyon of the same of your mother and father and nott of yourselffe."[7] As a counter to the rampant rationalism and madding intellects of an adult society teetering on the brink of heresy, Pole urges a childish humility whose warrant he derives directly from the Bible. "That Scripure itself doth signifie vnto vs to be furthest from wytt, and most vnlike to get things furth by dilligence of readeng, which be *paruuli*, that is to saye, lyttle babes," the Cardinal writes, for he "who wyll take fructe of Scripture other by readeng or heareng the wordes thereof, or ells by any declaration made thereupon, he must furst be made *paruulus*, without the whiche Scripture is not onelie vnprofitable but it is noysome and perniciouse."[8] As in these representative comments from Cardinal Pole, the topos of childhood, or "childship" as the cluster of values and attributes meant by the metaphoric use of childhood in Catholic discourse may be called, came to represent an attitude widely urged upon the faithful during the Counter Reformation.

As for the popularity of the topos in mid-century Tudor England, there are other, more speculative explanations for the upsurge of interest in both the state of childhood and its symbolic referents in Marian England. For the six years prior to Mary's ascension to the throne, England had had a child as its monarch, the boy-king Edward VI, Mary's young brother. During Somerset's regency and the subsequent period of Northumberland's influence, both the capacity of a child to rule and England's past history of youthful monarchs, from Richard II to Henry VI to the little Yorkist princes, must have been lively topics of alehouse conversation. For Mary herself, however, a Catholic princess in a Protestant land, the authority of her little brother was a far more pressing issue, for he and his counselors were determined that Mary, the presumptive heir, must forsake Catholicism in favor of reformed religion. Backed by the powerful support of her kinsman the Emperor Charles V, Mary evaded this requirement by adopting a theory put forth by Stephen Gardiner, bishop of Winchester and her future lord chancellor. As Jasper Ridley explains in his biography of Mary, Gardiner argued that "the royal absolute power over the Church could only be exercised by an adult king in person, and not by a regent on behalf of an infant king. He therefore argued that Somerset should not make any change in religion, but should leave things as they stood at Henry VIII's death, until Edward VI was old enough to decide for himself what he wished to do about religion."[9]

Edward's letters to his sister insisted that "we take our self for thadmyministracion of this commen welth, to haue ye same authoryty which our father had, diminished in no parte, neyther by example of scripture, nor by al universal lawes. The storyes of Scripture bee so plenteouse, as almoste the beste ordered church of the Isralites was by kings, younger then we bee."[10] But Mary steadfastly persisted in treating these letters as the work of unscrupulous counselors using her brother's authority for their own purposes. In brief, Mary herself had had direct and potentially dire involvement with current theories of childhood, its competence and constitution. This personal experience and her keen interest in the restoration of Catholicism in her reign may have countenanced and encouraged the view of childhood as a time of innocence and a state fit for humility and purity rather than adult concerns.[11]

Certainly Mary's co-religionists were quick to pick up the topos of childhood in the sermons, homilies, and celebrations designed to wean the populace from schismatic tenets back to the old faith. The chief spokesman of Marian Catholicism, Cardinal Pole, featured it prominently in his homilies, urging the English nation to accept the teachings of the Church as a child does his mother's lessons. Glancing back at the religious upheavals of the previous quarter-century, Pole implored Englishmen to now become *filij pacis*, children of peace, of grace, that each man must become "the chyld that hearing peace offered hym of the messenger of God, doeth giue eare vnto it, doth nott repugne to the same, but gladlier doth accept it."[12] The papal legate's preference for the "childship" image gave warrant to others to spread the need for a childlike trust and faith in the Church. Thus Leonard Pollard, prebendary of Worcester, in his *Fyue Homilies* (1556) likewise parallels the simplicity with which Christians should receive the teachings of the Church with children's instructions from their parents, while warning that the only way for us, "beinge but as babyes, and God's suckynge chyldren can be able to auoyde suche cruell daunger of that mischeuous beaste the deuyll: Verely if ye lyste to know it: other wayes is there none, then to keep us within the house of our father which is the Catholic Church."[13]

Meanwhile, children became both more prominent and more visible in the religious ceremonies and celebrations encouraged by the Marian authorities. From the first of Mary's reign, the children of St. Paul's, St. Anthony's, and the hospitals were incorporated into the processions and festivals with which London celebrated notable saints' days. The Tudor Diarist Henry Machyn observed the children of the queen's chapel singing mass in May 1554, and he is repeatedly impressed by such religious processions as that on St. Paul's day in January 1554/55 when he witnessed "a C. chylderyn in surples and a C. clarkes and prestes in copes syngyng, the wyche the copes wher very ryche of tyssure and cloth of gold," followed by the elevated sacrament, surrounded by twenty torches with two hundred men and

women bringing up the procession.[14] No less significant than
the inclusion of children in these various processions is the
fact that they customarily are described as *leading* the processions.

Like the religious ceremonies, royal entertainment at
court frequently featured children, especially in the dramatic
productions of Mary's reign. Easily the finest of these stage
plays is *Respublica* (ca. 1553), a well-constructed, lively, and
satirical interlude intended for court performance by boys.
So much modern critical attention has been paid to the play's
humorous assault on the social evils of the Reformation,
especially under Edward VI, that there is a danger the central
themes of *Respublica* may be overlooked. For all its topical
commentary, *Respublica* is a play about Obedience and Faith.
Lacking a sovereign guiding hand, Respublica, the state of
England, is easily deceived by the guile of Avarice and his
three cohorts, Insolence, Oppression, and Adulation, who
pretend to be Policy, Authority, and other desirable political
and civic virtues. The state is saved not through the recovery
of the true political virtues, however, but through prayer and
obedience. Hearing her prayers, God intercedes to aid Respublica, sending down the theological virtues Misericordia,
Pax, Justicia, and Verity to stand by Respublica, unmask the
false political virtues, and join the state to its proper head,
Nemesis, who is described in the prologue as a figure for
Queen Mary. Thus while they may come in time, it is not
political sagacity or expedience which will distinguish the
Marian state; rather reliance on the Scriptures, theological
principles, and divine guidance will enable England to over-
come her internal enemies and grow strong. As the example
of the long-suffering People in *Respublica* makes clear, what is
needed is belief in God's plan for England, faith in the
sovereign's commitment to bring the plan to fruition, and a
due obedience to superior authority. Thus, as David Bev-

ington points out, the play teaches that "strong, unquestioned single rule can provide the only safeguard. The queen figure in Act V of *Respublica* is no umpire. . . . Nemesis (Mary), who is herself a goddess, listens only to the voice of divine guidance. The insistence on royal absolutism sanctioned by providence is thus a political deterrent to the theory of rule by human counsel."[15]

As avatars of the simple faith of childhood, the children of the church schools were a perfect choice for a play about Obedience and Faith. *Respublica* is almost surely the work of the Tudor schoolmaster Nicholas Udall and, as W.W. Greg argues, this is probably the play intended for performance at the coronation festivities for Queen Mary in October 1553.[16] For whatever reason it was put back until Christmastime, the play's performance at court in December 1553 must mark one of the earliest invocations of childship in the young Marian era. The child speaking the prologue makes clear the rationale for children appearing in a dramatic entertainment to instruct their elders:

But shall boyes (saith some nowe) of suche highe mattiers plaie?
No not as discussers, but yet the booke dothe saie
Ex ore infantium perfecisti Laudem,
for whan Criste came rydinge into *Hieresalem,*
The yong babes with tholde folke cryed owte all & some,
blessed bee the man that in the Lordes name dothe come.
Soo for goode Englande sake this presente howre & daie
In hope of hir restoring from hir late decaye,
we children to youe olde folke, both with harte, & voyce
maie Ioyne all togither to thanke god & Reioyce
That he hath sent Marye our Soveraigne & Quene
to reforme thabuses which hitherto hath been,

. . . .

Leat vs booth yong & olde to godde commend her grace[17]

[39-56]

Hence the propriety of children, symbols of innocence and faith, to introduce, perform, and interpret a play on the themes of Obedience and Faith in the state.

Within the play, the lesson of childship must be learned by the protagonist, Respublica, paradoxically a mother who must recover childlike qualities again. Her people come to her begging for succor and relief, but her only active attempt to alleviate their distress is her disastrous scheme to rely solely on the vices disguised as virtues. This action fails utterly and Respublica is so blinded by her error that despite five years of the vices' misrule, punctuated by the pointed complaints of her ministers by People, she still fails to realize her mistake. Instead, desperate, she turns to prayer and complete dependence on God. Her faith is rewarded when God sends his children, traditionally the "Four Daughters of God" from Psalm 85 (Mercy, Truth, Justice, and Peace), to enlighten Respublica, capture the vices for her, and introduce her to Nemesis, the sovereign appointed by God to guide her destiny under His watchful eye. Thus, as People looks to Respublica for their safety and succor, she in turn looks to her sovereign who initiates civic action in accord with God's will. The central lesson, then, is that of obedience within the hierarchical order of the state, an order which, the play makes clear, flows ultimately from God through the monarch to the state and its people. Insofar as this is a political message, it is best articulated by child actors whose presence is a reminder of the virtues of simple faith and obedience.

While preachers and homilists thus urged childship upon the country and playwrights explored its dramatic possibilities, Mary's ministers moved to resurrect and reinstitute the one great festival of the medieval Church given over to the celebration of childhood, the traditional Childermass ceremonies, with all their accretions of St. Nicholas and Child Bishop traditions. Under Mary, these popular Christmastide celebrations became the center of the renewed interest in childhood and the ripest symbol of the Catholic conception of childship as a social and religious ideal. Mary became queen in late summer of 1553 and, at the urging of her advisors, at first moved deliberately and circumspectly toward the reinstitution of Catholicism in England. But by the following year there was no doubt about her intentions, and by the fall of 1554 plans were in the works to celebrate Childermass, always a popular feast, in the old fashion. In London, on November 13, 1554, Bishop Edmund Bonner issued an official order allowing all clerks in London to go abroad and have St. Nicholas in the old manner on December 6. Although the order was countermanded at the last moment, perhaps as E.K. Chambers suggests because Cardinal Pole had appointed the saint's day for a great feast of reconciliation at Lambeth,[18] clerks in several of the London parishes proceeded to go abroad singing, wassailing, and celebrating. Subsequently, the children's festivities, beginning on St. Nicholas's Day, December 6, climaxing on Holy Innocents' Day, December 28, and continuing in some sections of the country all the way to Candlemas in early February, were celebrated until at the death of Mary England returned to Protestantism and the festivities were abandoned.[19]

Henry VIII had abolished the Childermass ceremonies in 1541 in a proclamation which held up the ceremonies as a symbol of lewd and foolish papist rites. And Bishop Gardiner, in the *Articles* put to him in 1550, was required to affirm "that the counterfeiting St. Nicholas, St. Clement, St. Catherine and St. Edmund, by children, heretofore brought into the church, was a mockery and foolishness."[20] Now, with Henry's daughter on the throne and dedicated to bringing the country back to Catholicism, the ceremonies were revived both as popular festivities that reminded the people of the holiday traditions of the Church and as the proper forum for a further exposition of the childship topos. The Marian authorities particularly wished to revive such ceremonies as the cluster of Christmastide children's festivities as a means of linking mid-Tudor England with an idealized vision of a medieval merry Catholic England, united socially and religiously. However mythical this vision of unity and harmony in fact was, it proved an excellent tool for reminding the populace that it was the Reformers who preached and nurtured divisiveness in church and state. And the revival of popular old ceremonies, such as the Childermass Boy Bishop's procession and sermon, helped underscore a key doctrinal point, that the Scriptures alone were not enough for salvation; the ritual, ceremonies, and traditions of the Church, even when they appeared childish or foolish (and what of man's does not in God's perspective?), were necessary for well-ordered Christian life.

As we have seen in Chapter 2, the Salisbury Processional and Breviary offer a clear picture of the Childermass ceremonies as practiced in England.[21] The choir boys or schoolboys assumed for twenty-four hours the rights, duties, and privileges of their elders in the performance of religious services. A Boy Bishop and his retinue processed to the altar on a chapel, discharged ritual duties, and returned to the choir until Vespers on Childermass Day. After having performed duties for that day (including a sermon but probably not mass) and having taken dinner, the procession went through the streets on horseback, accepting gifts and levying contributions. Later various entertainments were held. But the privileges of the Boy Bishop and his charges usually extended to Candlemas, February 2, and they continued to travel about the parish or country being feted and receiving contributions from citizens, churches, and institutions in the area.[22]

Only one of the Boy Bishop's sermons survives from the Marian period. When compared with the other two surviving Tudor Boy Bishops' sermons, the Marian one, of which some account has been given in Chapter 2, echoes the themes and general characteristics of the type. The chief significant differences between the Marian sermon and its predecessors are the stress on the symbolic nature of childship and the topicality of the references to current events in the Marian sermon, which was delivered in 1558 during the brief period between the death of Queen Mary and the coronation of Elizabeth.[23] It contains a full explication of the childship topos recurrent in Marian Catholic literature, beginning with an explication of the classical Scriptural text in praise of children, Christ's admonition to his apostles in Matthew 18 that "Except you will be convertyd, and make lyke unto lytill children, you shall not entre in to the kingdom of heaven." The Biblical context of the quotation, the apostles squabbling among themselves over which should be first in the heavenly kingdom, in its rebuke of contention and pride in favor of meekness, lowliness, and humility, had an obvious application to faction-ridden mid-Tudor England.

The speaker warns against a too literal application of Christ's injunction, stressing the symbolic and figurative construction that must be placed on Jesus' words in praise of childishness, a warning that we look to its "sprite" rather than letter. Christ is not advocating "a miraculous or monstruose conversion of a man in to a childe as touching age, stature, and discretion, but of a moral conversion, as touching certyn evill manners that are reprovyd in men, and other contrary maners which are comendyd in childer, by which means it is possible ynough for the greatest of men to becum as litill childer, and for the eldest of women to becum in lyknes of maners as young babes, which are symple, without gyle, innocent, wythowt harme, and all pure wythowt corruption, as few above the age of childer are, and as all ought to be" (p. 15). Here then is childship as a symbolic cluster of mental and moral attitudes which "litill ones have by nature" (p. 16) but which adults must work to possess. This the speaker describes as his theme, the proper change "of men into childer" (p. 19). The key to this metamorphosis is the master virtue of Innocence, and thus the Boy Bishop urges both children and adults in his audience "specially, and among all other vertues, I wold wish yow to embrace the innocency of childer, for that one vertue includeth all, as the generall includeth the speciall, for who that hath this innocency hath halfe the rightuousness and perfection of a Christian man's lyfe" (pp. 21-22). This special virtue of children is the intuitive and instinctive love of goodness as embodied in the Church, a love as strong and automatic in the true Christian as the infant's love for its parents. The antithesis of this innocency would then be experience, in particular experimentation with the lures of a secular world filled with "new fanglyd doctrine" (p. 21). Innocence, the capstone of the childship topos, is the concept which underlies and coordinates the parts of the Boy Bishop's sermon. It forms a bridge, for example, into the first major division of the sermon, a discussion of martyrdom and the qualities by which a true martyr might be known, a topic made urgent by the still smoldering fires of Smithfield.

The sermon follows the initial survey of Biblical texts relating to children and childhood with a section on the memorial function of the feast, the commemoration of the original slaughter of the innocents by Herod. The audience is reminded not only of the purity and innocence of these little martyrs, but also of their prerogative as the first martyrs for Christ, and also their uniqueness in dying not only for the spirit and faith of Christ but also for His body, giving their lives in place of His. They are distinguished by their "pure innocency," which further serves to set them off from those who "are far wyde of true martirdom, and consequently of the kyngdom too, which suffryd violence of fyre, hangyng, headyng, banysshyng, or other just execution, for many and divers enormities in ther faith and maners . . . lackyng the commendacion of innocency, which unto martirdom, as I said, is a vertue most necessary" (p. 17). Childship then becomes a touchstone for distinguishing true from pseudo-martyrs, thereby excluding those Protestants who mimic the behavior but lack the spirit of "all the martirs that ever were alowyd and approvyd for trew and holy Martyrs [who] in dede were all Innocentes, giltles of ther death, by no means deservyng the same on ther owne behalfe" (p. 18).

The body of the Gloucester sermon consists of serial addresses to the respective groups making up the Boy Bishop's audience, adults, children, and schoolmasters, explaining to each the importance of incorporating childship into their lives. For the first group, "I gather this lesson for yow that are of the elder sort, that of necessitie you must nede reforme your corrupt maners, which are dissonant and disagreable with the incorrupt maners of childer" (p. 20); for Christ's answer to his apostles shows "that the kyngdom of heavyn wold not be gotten by pride, ambition, contencion, envy, emulacion, stowtness, and elacion; therfor they abasyd them selves to most profound humilitie, povertie, mekeness of spirite; and convertyd ther maners most like to the maners of innocent childer" (p. 20).

At this point, having set forth the paradigm of childship as a goal to be sought for all, the author makes a central distinction between the ideal of innocence and mere childishness basic to the Marian concept of childship. There are certain aspects of childhood such as frivolity, ignorance, and the like, which are to be avoided; thus the Boy Bishop explains, properly understood, the Scripture enjoins us "Not to be childysh in witt, understandyng, and discrecion" (pp. 20-21). Here an interesting and important distinction is made between the positive and negative dimensions of childhood, a clarification of the distance between symbol and reality, the ideal pattern and real English children. The speaker is well aware of the unruly, less attractive side of childhood, of all the negative connotations of childishness. From this point of view, it is

a childysh poynt for any Christian man to waver in his faith, and that it is for lak of witt if he be caried from the doctrine of his awncient relligion in to a new fanglyd doctrine, which hath no suertie in it, but is inconstant as the wynd. Yf this be a childysh poynt, and argueth lak of witt and discrecion, as S. Pawl saith, I report me to you how many witless childer and childysh people were in thys realme of late years and yet are in many places, which waveryd in ther faith, and were caried hyder and thyder, from one opinion to another, as childer ar caried with an apple, or wyth a puffe of wynd, as thei that have strength to resist nothing, which is reproveable in men that should have constancie and discrecion. [p. 21]

The careful distinction between childship and mere childishness thus allows the Catholic writer to use both views of childhood to castigate heretics.

Childship as a symbolic cluster of moral virtues, the greatest of which is innocence, is strengthened rather than undercut by the recognition that real childhood contains undesirable traits along with attractive ones. The Marian writer has no difficulty explaining and distinguishing a key topos which may be employed as a positive goal while noting its incongruence with the frequently unruly children of his audience's experience. These real English children he turns to after his lecture to the adults and, in one of the most delightful portions of the sermon, seeks in the children (both "boys and wenches") assembled before him for a fit living, breathing exemplar of childship. However, the task, he finds, is more difficult than one might expect for, he laments, "it is wonder to me to se amonge yow so many childer in years, and so few innocentes in maners" (p. 23). Exaggerating for polemical effect, and with a deft use of humor to leaven his message, the Boy Bishop considers sequentially the children of the city, of the grammar schools, and finally the choristers and children of the Song School, discovering each to be corrupt, despite cherubic outward appearances: "Loke in his face and yow wold think that butter wold not melt in his mouth; but, as smothe as he lokes, I will not wysh yow to folow hym if yow know as much as I do. Well, well! all is not gold that shynes, nor all are not innocentes that beare the face of childer" (p. 25). In fact, for an uncorrupted exemplar, the Boy Bishop finally must settle for an infant too young to run away from its mother's hand. And as further evidence of the need for strict curbs on the behavior of youth, the sermon continues with an attack on permissive parents and a defense of corporal punishment. Thus, the symbol of childship is distinguished from the actual class with which it originated.

As the fullest surviving explication of a key topos in mid-Tudor Catholic thought, the Gloucester Boy Bishop's sermon is both a remarkable and an important document. It demonstrates the potential for this central concept, which I have called childship, to function as both a symbol or emblem of the qualities needed for Christian living in a world of turmoil and as a weapon against heresy and deception. The knowledge it affords us of the full ramifications of the topos of childhood should enrich our appreciation of the image of childhood in Tudor thought and art.

Finally, the success of the Catholic use of childship may be judged in part by the reactions of Protestant writers to it. Such sturdy Reformers as John Foxe and George Puttenham digressed from other topics to assail the Marian Childermass ceremonies which apotheosized the ideal, and the Anglican Church's most effective Elizabethan spokesman, Richard Hooker, lamented that "an opinion hath spread it selfe very farre in the world, as if the way to be ripe in faith, were to be raw in wit and judgement; as if reason were an enemy vnto Religion, childish simplicitie the mother of ghostly, and divine wisedom."[24] Such hostile testimony bears witness to the effectiveness of the topos of childship in English Counter Reformation literature, a topos most sharply defined and widely disseminated in England during the reign of Mary Tudor.

FIVE

John Foxe's *Book of Martyrs* and the Child Reader

John Foxe's *Book of Martyrs* (1563) figures in almost every history of children's literature because, for three centuries, it was regularly placed in the hands of Protestant children in England and the colonies by generations of pious parents.[1] Rev. John Milner's mid-Victorian recollection is a representative testimony to the place of Foxe's horrific annals in English childhood: "Foxe's martyrs are among our earliest recollections, and their spirit-stirring incidents riveted our eyes to their pages in our earliest childhood. Here we see 'the great things that faith can do and the great things that faith can suffer.' Here we behold, in fact, what Bunyan has so admirably described in fiction; here is Faithful again suffering and dying."[2] Foxe and Bunyan: both are food for tender palates. The original Renaissance editions, massive black folios, were expensive; but, by government decree, chained in cathedral and many parish churches and laid out in the anterooms and chambers of many an ecclesiastic, they were as readily accessible to children as to their elders.[3] Later, beginning in the sixteenth century, literally hundreds of

Proceedings of the Ninth Annual Conference of the Children's Literature Association (1983), pp. 147-56

abridgments of Foxe's book brought the purchase price of the work within the budget of every godly household. There is, then, no question of the enormous popularity of the book or of the regular practice of encouraging children to read it.[4] What does want closer examination is the type of appeal and likely effect of Foxe's book upon the youthful reader. More specifically, is there any evidence that Foxe was conscious of a juvenile audience, that he attempted to reach such an audience through special appeals or strategems—in brief, has the *Book of Martyrs* any claim to be a book designed, at least in part, for the consumption of young readers? Might it be truly a children's book by design and execution as well as by historical accident? This chapter will address these questions and attempt to prove that a juvenile readership was a particular conscious target of Foxe.

As discussed in Chapter 1, the first two editions of the work which became the *Book of Martyrs* were written and published abroad in Latin, but the great *Actes and Monuments of These Latter and Perillous Dayes* . . . (1563) was produced in the vulgar tongue for the explicit benefit of "the simple flock of Christ, especially the unlearned sort, so miserably abused." Foxe aimed at reaching all classes and all ages. The book proceeds by various strategies to exert mass appeal, and it is these techniques which have subsequently come to be most closely associated with the field of children's literature.

First, there is Foxe's method. Although he wrote of theological matters (and the title *Book of Martyrs* is a popular one never used by Foxe himself, who preferred the more formal *Acts and Monuments* or *Ecclesiastical History* [1570]), Foxe rejected the style of the tract or sermon for narrative and description of heroic and tragic action. The stories of the Protestant martyrs function as an emblem to refute the errors of Rome. Further, his *Book of Martyrs* is replete with lavish woodcuts, perhaps based on his own original sketches, coordinated with his text, and amplified as the popularity of the book occasioned additional printings. The extensive use of illustrations, more than 160 in the second English edition of 1570, extends the range of appeal of Foxe's book even to illiterate laborers and housewives and, more significant to us, to the preliterate audience of children from toddlers to apprentices, as I have noted before. Indeed, the major themes of the book are clear from the woodcuts, which are often grouped in sets without reference to the text. These illustrations elicit strong emotional reactions regardless of one's age, status, or sophistication.[5]

For those in grammar school or who had their alphabets and some modest skill in reading, Foxe appended another aid to the basic text of the *Book of Martyrs*. In the margins of the English editions appear running scholia which function as an often robust guide to the frequent involutions of Foxe's material. Here Foxe offers not only a shorthand guide to the text but a commentary, simple, pithy, and often humorous, on the events and issues discoursed at greater length on the page. For example, Foxe discusses the origins of monastic practices, reproducing a medieval epistle arguing that monks should shave their heads as evidence of their humility and solemn vows. Foxe's terse gloss, "Much sayd, nothing proved" (1:10), cuts through the intricacies of the argument. A Catholic disquisition on the power claimed by bishops to free souls from purgatory is awarded a laconic gloss by Foxe: "Like a pulled hen" (2:7). Pithy, colloquial, direct, these marginal scholia are readily accessible to such inexperienced readers as children, cutting a quick, humorous swath through difficult or turgid sections. The scholia may thus represent, like the engravings, another attempt by Foxe to extend the range and appeal of his book to every audience.

Another technique utilized by Foxe to press home his themes to the broadest possible readership is repetition of words, action, and ideas. It is probably safe to say that no one ever sat down and read the *Book of Martyrs* straight through (the Elizabethan editions ran over two thousand folio pages; the last complete modern edition totaled over six thousand); instead, it is a book to be read and studied piecemeal, over a period of time. With this circumstance in mind, Foxe focussed on the key issues which divided Roman Catholicism from Protestantism and the dissenting tradition from which it emerged: the nature of the Eucharist, for example, and the role of the priesthood in general and the Bishop of Rome in particular. Thus, the central issues are much the same wherever the reader opens Foxe's book, whether in the reign of the Emperor Constantine or King John or Mary Tudor; Foxe's habit of repetition and stress upon key issues immediately orients the reader. Similarly, the patterns of examination, torture, and martyrdom vary only in minor detail according to age and location; the larger meaning of the individual Christian dying for his faith is constant. This repetition is a key technique for Foxe; it enables him to connect the suffering and sacrifice of sixteenth-century Protestants with those of dissenters and reformers through the Middle Ages, back to the Roman arenas, and finally to the apostles themselves. The Tudor Protestants are thus seen to be not a schismatic sect newly sprung up to battle Mother Church but rather the true apostolic church, keeping alive the religion of the Bible forsaken by the degenerate Roman church.

Once children were directed to Foxe's book by conscientious parents who wished their offspring to learn the history and heroes of their faith, with appropriate moral lessons, they found a work no less accessible than exciting, a compilation of riveting stories of sturdy Christian heroes pitted against black-hearted tyrants and persecutors. In fact, much of the *Book of Martyrs* reads like a good melodrama with vivid heroes, almost Old Testament figures, standing firm upon the faith against the threats and blandishments of such treacherous, potent, and godless villains as Turks, Jews, assorted heathen, and, worst of all, Antichrist and his minions (identified early in the book as the Pope and the Catholic religious orders). The old black-letter folios fall open readily to the dogeared pages containing the horrific and inspirational deaths of Latimer, Ridley, Hooper, and the other heroes of the Marian persecution.

No less spine-tingling are the larger than life villains, "wily Winchester," "bloody Bonner," and their tribe. Indeed Foxe occasionally becomes so caught up in describing these persecutors that they come across less as historical figures than as caricatures or cartoon villains in the comic book vein. For example, in recounting Bishop Bonner's method of personally scourging unfortunate Protestants, especially children, in his garden, Foxe tells the story of one youth whom Bonner could not drive to recant his faith through whipping: "Oftimes speaking of the same John Milles, he would say 'They call me bloody Bonner. A vengeance on you all! I would fain be rid of you, but you have a delight in burning. But if I might have my will, I would sew your mouths, and put you in sacks, and drown you!' " (8:486). Such passages may make dubious history, but they are fine propaganda, guaranteed to send a shudder down the spine of an impressionable reader at this confirmation of Bonner's monstrosity from his own mouth.

The stories themselves are often masterful. Helen C. White justly calls Foxe "a storyteller of quite remarkable power, one of the greatest of a great age."[6] Indeed, so many of his stories have passed into English mythology that the average modern reader, even one ignorant of Foxe, knows

Mary Tudor as "Bloody Mary," recalls Latimer's final encour-
agement to Ridley at the stake to "Be of good comfort, master
Ridley, and play the man. We shall this day light such a
candle, by God's grace, in England, as I trust shall never be
put out," and generally views the Marian era through the
ideological lens constructed and popularized by Foxe. Thus,
Foxe's skill at characterization, or caricature, his habit of
simplifying and clarifying moral issues, and, of course, his
storytelling facility attracted youthful readers as readily as
their elders.

Thus far, I have been considering aspects of Foxe's artistry
in the *Book of Martyrs* which would have had a particular
appeal to a juvenile audience. The more specific question yet
remains, however; did Foxe consciously intend a juvenile
readership and tailor his craftsmanship to the needs and
interests of that segment of his audience? I think an examination of his treatment of children in the *Book of Martyrs* will
confirm that he did target this audience. One of the most
striking pieces of evidence of this concern with youthful
readers appears in a story Foxe added to the second edition of
his book, a story in which he speaks directly to his young
readers. Here is the story Foxe tells:

God's punish-
ment upon a
damsel of
twelve years
old.

The same William Maldon, chanced afterward
to dwell at a town six miles from London, called
Walthamstow, where his wife taught young children
to read, which was about the year of our Lord 1563,
and the fourth year of queen Elizabeth's reign. Unto
this school, amongst other children came one Benfield's daughter named Dennis, about the age of
twelve years.

As these children sat talking together, they happened among other talk (as the nature of children is
to be busy with many things) to fall into communi-

cation of God, and to reason among themselves, after their childish discretion, what he should be. Whereunto some answered one thing, some another. Among whom, when one of the children had said, that he was a good old Father; the foresaid Dennis Benfield, casting out impious words of horrible blasphemy, "What! he," said she, "is an old doting fool."

What wretched and blasphemous words were these, ye hear. Now mark what followed. When William Maldon heard of these abominable words of the girl, he willed his wife to correct her for the same: which was appointed the next day to be done. But when the next morrow came, her mother would needs send her to the market to London, the wench greatly entreating her mother that she might not go, being marvellously unwilling thereunto. Howbeit, through her mother's compulsion, she was forced to go, and went. And what happened? Her business being done at London, as she was returning again homeward, and being a little past Hackney, suddenly the young girl was so stricken, that all the one side of her was black, and she speechless. Whereupon immediately she was carried back to Hackney, and there the same night was buried.—The witness of the same story was William Maldon and his wife; also Benfield her father, and her mother, which yet be all alive.

A terrible example, no doubt, both to young and old, what it is for children to blaspheme the Lord their God, and what it is for parents to suffer their young ones to grow up in such blasphemous blindness, and not to nurture them betimes in the rudiments of the Christian catechism, to know first their creation, and then their redemption in Christ our Saviour, to fear the name of God, and to reverence

Blasphemy punished.

his majesty. For else what do they deserve but to be taken away by death, which contemptuously despise him, of whom they take the benefit of life?

A lesson to children and young girls.

And therefore let all young maids, boys, and young men, take example by this wretched silly wench, not only [not] to blaspheme the sacred majesty of the omnipotent God their creator, but also not one to take his name in vain, according as they are taught in his commandments.   [8:640]

Notice that the marginal gloss no less than the text itself speaks to a juvenile audience. Further, Foxe uses the child as exemplar for adults, cautioning, "For if this young maiden, who was not fully twelve years old, for her irreverent speaking of God (and that but at one time), did not escape the stroke of God's terrible hand, what then have they to look for, which, being men grown in years and stricken in age, being so often warned and preached unto, yet cease not continually with their blasphemous oaths, not only to abuse his name, but also most contumeliously and despitefully to tear him (as it were), and all his parts in pieces?" (8:641).

The story of the unfortunate little Dennis Benfield may serve as a prototype for Foxe's handling of children in the *Book of Martyrs*. They do not appear simply to swell the throng in his great collection but rather, as with the twelve-year-old blasphemer, to serve an exemplary function, either positive or negative, aimed at teaching right conduct directly to the child reader and, by analogy and extension, to the adult reader. Thus with children as with adults, Foxe's bipolar vision divides them into two opposed camps, the godly children and their wicked brethren. The godly obey and succor their elders, follow the Christian precepts they have been taught, and are inspirational models for adults who lack their purity, innocence, and childish conviction of the ultimate triumph of goodness.

Among the inspirational stories of godly children, two from the Roman persecutions of the fourth century are particularly notable. In one, Eulalia, a twelve-year-old Portuguese girl, is so offended at a command that all Christians must sacrifice to idols that she steals away from the country house where her parents, worried at her excess of zeal, have sequestered her and makes her way to the city square where she finds the judge and officers attending the idols. Little Eulalia marches up and delivers a stirring speech condemning not only the false idols but also the emperor. The judge attempts to calm her and urges she consider the matter. "To this Eulalia made no answer, but being in a great fury, she spitteth in the tyrant's face; she throweth down the idols, and spurneth abroad with her feet the heap of incense prepared to the censers" (1:271). At this point torture proceeds until Eulalia expires while singing a hymn.

In another instance, a Christian stalwart, Romanes, is preaching a sermon while being flayed alive by torturers. The captain of the guard complains in frustration that he is unable to break Romanes, who replies that even a child, free of deceit, can tell who the true God is. On the spot, a child is then hauled up by the captain from the crowd watching the execution. The youth, seven years of age, affirms the Christian faith, which he says he learned from his mother. This lady is then called up on the scaffolding and interrogated while the child is "horsed up" and scourged; the mother remains calm, rebuking the lad once for calling for water and reminding him to remember little Isaac. Finally, the torturer scalps the child, but the mother assures the boy that God will give him a crown to cover his naked head, which so encourages the child that he receives more stripes "with a smiling countenance." Finally, the captain, unable to break the child either, commits him to "stinking prison" while he finishes off

Romanes, after which the boy is brought back out and beheaded while his mother sings a hymn. Foxe comments approvingly on this edifying tale in his gloss which calls it "An example of vertuous education" (1:261).

Many examples of virtuous and godly children are less sensational, but closer to the experience of Elizabethan youth. There are the godly children of Merindol in France, for example. In 1542, papal examiners discovered that the townsfolk of Merindol had been reading their Bibles for themselves and arrived at a pure Protestant faith which they had taught even their youngest children. Foxe devotes several pages to an account of how the small children astounded the examiners by the thoroughness with which they had their catechisms and the wholeness of their faith (4:494ff).

In England, to take a native example, when John Lawrence was burned for his faith at Colchester in the 1550s, his legs had been so chafed and rotted by the prison irons that he had to be brought to the stake in a chair. At this pathetic spectacle, Foxe relates, "young children came about the fire, and cried, as well as young children could speak, saying, 'Lord, strengthen thy servant, and keep thy promise; Lord, strengthen thy servant, and keep thy promise:' which thing, as it is rare, so it is no small manifestation of the glory of God, who wrought this in the hearts of these little ones; nor yet a little commendation to their parents, who, from their youth, brought them up in knowledge of God and his truth" (6:740).

One final example of the godly child as object of emulation for youthful readers comes from the story of Rawlins White, an illiterate Welsh fisherman martyred during the Marian persecution. Dissatisfied with the Catholic religion, White sent his small son to school to learn to read so that the child could read to his father from the Bible. This the dutiful boy did, "a special minister appointed by God, no doubt, for that purpose," Foxe remarks, converting his father to the Protestant faith (7:29).

Negative examples of childish behavior, such as the twelve-year-old blasphemer, are also plentiful in the *Book of Martyrs*. Especially chilling are the stories of children who informed to the Catholic authorities on their parents. During the reign of Henry VIII, for example, one John Colins of Burford impeached his own father, Thomas, to the Bishop. Foxe records that "the crime against Thomas Colins was, that for the eight years past this Thomas Colins the father had taught this John his son, in the presence of his mother, the Ten Commandments, and namely, that he should have but one God, and should worship but God alone; and that to worship saints, and go on pilgrimage, was idolatry. Also, that he should not worship the sacrament of the altar as God, for that it was but a token of the Lord's body: which thing so much discontented this John Colins, that he said he would disclose his father's errors, and make him to be burned; but his mother entreated him not so to do" (4:236). Foxe condemns not only John Colins the perfidious son, but he also inveighs against "the blind ignorance and uncourteous dealing of the bishops" who "constrained the children to accuse their parents" (4:240). The savagery of sinful children is evident in various other stories, as in two separate and unrelated stories of schoolboys who torture and then murder their schoolmasters for teaching them Christian principles (1:268-70, 2:31).

Finally, Foxe makes clear to his youthful Protestant audience what, in particular, they have to fear from the traditional enemies of the true faith. Following his account of the close of the Roman persecutions, Foxe focusses on two classes of pagan enemies of Christianity, the bloody Turks and the impious Jews. Although Foxe is not notably anti-Semitic by the standards of his age, in recounting the alleged atrocities committed by English Jews in the Middle Ages, he manages to repeat various stories of Jews capturing and whipping Christian children preparatory to crucifying them on Good Friday as a horrible mockery of Christianity. Foxe justifies a twelfth-century pogrom in York on these grounds, affirms the crucifixion in Lincoln of a nine-year-old lad, and tells a story of a Norwich boy seized, circumcised, and held for months by Jews planning to crucify him on Good Friday (2:534). Horrifying as the prospect of crucifixion might be, however, when Foxe comes to discuss the Turks' treatment of Christian children, it is apparent that there are worse fates than death. Captured children, Foxe relates, are forced to renounce Christ, brought up as Muslims, and pressed into the dreadful Janizzaries whose primary purpose is to slay Christians. "What a lamentable thing is it," Foxe exclaims, "to see and behold our own children, born of our own bodies, to become our mortal and cruel enemies, and to cut our throats with their own hands! This servitude of mind is far greater than death itself" (4:36). As usual in Foxe when one thinks he has reached the ultimate horror, there is more. If the captured Christian children are physically attractive, rather than being forced into the Janizzaries, they are instead "compelled to serve their abominable abomination; and when age cometh, then they serve instead of eunuchs" (4:84).

All of this should certainly give a normal child reader chills, if not nightmares, but there was the consolation that Jews were banished from England and the Turks were far across the seas. The present, immediate enemy was instead the Antichrist at Rome and his legions, including the fifth column of Elizabethan Catholics who had so recently held power in England—and might again if anything should happen to Queen Elizabeth. The youthful reader learns as early as Foxe's preface that the religious orders are natural enemies of children, regular practitioners of infanticide, the natural consequence, Foxe observes, of forcing priests and nuns to live "sole, without matrimony" (1:xiii). Nevertheless, they do have a use for children; like the Turks, the holy orders need youth to swell their ranks and thus, Foxe suggests, friars steal men's children to make them of their sect (2:358). Meanwhile, Foxe includes assorted stories of godly children suffering at the hands of Catholic inquisitors, especially Bishop Bonner, a particular bogeyman for children, and recounts stories of boys and girls forced to light the fires that consumed their parents at the stake (e.g., 4:245).

Because most children, including Foxe's youthful readers, are not of the heroic mold of little Eulalia and are relatively powerless in an adult society which denies them even minimal rights, it is stories such as these latter, of children being forced to commit terrible acts or falling victim not through any heroic bent toward martyrdom but through the random savagery of Catholic rule as Foxe portrays it, that would have moved Renaissance children most powerfully. As Foxe describes the Catholic state, there is in it no security, no rest for the faithful Christian. Among the stories Foxe tells of Bishop Bonner's dealings with children, two make this point sharply. Foxe devotes several pages to the pathetic story of an eight-year-old boy who goes to the Bishop's house to try to see his father, who is being held there for interrogation by Bonner. The Bishop orders his priests to seize and scourge the child and then to deliver him in that condition to his father. The reunion of father and son is one of the most pathetic scenes in Foxe. Within two weeks, Foxe reports, the child died of the beating (7:510-12). Another story concerns "a child that passed not the age of 15 years" who came into Bishop Bonner's hands because, without understanding their meaning, he repeated words he had heard from others against the sacrament. (5:442) His terrified confessions were disallowed, his parents were barred from interceding or even visiting their son, and, at the stake, he frantically praised the Bishop and offered to say anything Bonner wished; all was to no avail and the burning proceeded.

As these stories indicate, the child in the grip of Catholic authorities is utterly powerless, beyond the aid of friends or parents. Parents could also be carried off without notice, turning the child's life upside down. Foxe relates the story of one Marian martyr whose brave death at the stake left a wife and three young children behind. Seizing the opportunity, the local lord of the district confiscated all the goods of the family and hounded the widow and her children out of town (8:463). Perhaps we can gauge the effect of the continual uncertainty and dread on the child reader, the possibility of instant disruption of the family unit inspired by the reign of terror which Catholic dominance brought, by noting its effect on children within the *Book of Martyrs*. In telling the story of another Marian martyr, John Rough, a particular target of Bishop Bonner because Rough maintained that he had himself travelled to Rome, seen the Pope, and knew him to be the real Antichrist, Foxe describes how Bonner sent officers to arrest him. Describing the taking of Rough in his house, Foxe mentions that he had a two-year-old daughter, Rachel, who shared his bed. The child had been afflicted for some time with nightmares, Foxe explains, of her father being dragged from the bed and taken away at night (8:455). One can imagine the effect on the child of seeing her worst nightmares come true.

The overwritten villainies of Bonner and the bloodthirsty Catholic officials and the heroic sacrifices of Eulalia, Tyndale, Latimer, and the rest doubtless stirred children; but I suspect it was the atmosphere of terror, the knowledge that nothing was sacred, nothing secure, not even the family unit nor the parental bed, that sunk most deeply into the psyches of Foxe's youthful readers. This was just Foxe's design and purpose: to so convince Englishmen of every age and station of the unmitigated horror of Catholic dominion that they would resist to the death any attempt to reintroduce that religion into England. His success may be measured by the hundreds of editions and reprints of his book from the sixteenth to the twentieth centuries, including, in our time, a vividly illustrated color comic book version published by the Protestant Truth Society for the special consumption of children. Foxe thought his message universal, timeless, and directly relevant to every Christian regardless of age; and, as I have sought to demonstrate here, in particular he tailored his great book for the interests and capacities of the young readers who would one day have to preserve England from the powers of darkness.

SIX

Michael Drayton's *Nymphidia*: A Children's Classic?

The major difficulty encountered in discussing children's nonacademic reading during the Renaissance is that little, if any, children's literature as such (books, as F.J.H. Darton puts it, "which would openly allow a child to enjoy himself with no thought of duty nor fear of wrong")[1] was published prior to the eighteenth century. Yet long before they became a distinct object of the book trade, English children read avidly of whatever literature was available to them, and in the process they made some adult books—*Pilgrim's Progress, Robinson Crusoe, Gulliver's Travels* are all familiar instances—their own. But of the various kinds of ostensibly adult literature to which children have been drawn, the fairy tale has endured as the most popular.

Early evidence of this affinity is sparse but tantalizing. In *The Tatler* (No. 95: 1709) Richard Steele describes a visit to the home of his eight-year-old godson. The boy had abandoned Aesop to immerse himself in medieval and Renaissance chivalric romances. As for the boy's little sister, Steele writes that "the mother told me, 'that . . . Betty . . . deals

Children's Literature: Annual of the Modern Language Association Group on Children's Literature and the Children's Literature Association 6 (Philadelphia: Temple University Press, 1977), 34-41

chiefly in fairies and sprights.' "[2] What had the little girl, who according to her mother was a better scholar than her brother, been reading of fairy lore? One critic speculates that "it seems likely that these fairies and sprites were of native origin."[3] Another suggests, "she may possibly have come upon *Nymphidia* or Spenser or browsed among the poets."[4]

Michael Drayton's *Nymphidia* (published in 1627) has been justly called "the finest of all seventeenth-century fantasies."[5] Critical consensus no longer considers the prolific Drayton a major Renaissance poet.[6] It is nevertheless true, as his modern editor remarks, that "*Nymphidia* has won wider and more continued popularity than any other poem of Drayton's."[7] I suggest that much of the sustained popularity of Drayton's fairy poem lies in its particular appeal to children, and I propose to analyze the elements in the poem which contribute to this appeal.

Like his Warwickshire countryman William Shakespeare, Drayton was originally a country boy, widely read but without university training, who made his mark in London as a poet of talent and versatility. And again like his friend Shakespeare, Drayton appears to have written for the widest possible popular audience. Thus in the early seventeenth century, while Donne and the metaphysical poets wrote for and circulated manuscripts among an avant-garde intellectual coterie and Jonson and the Tribe of Ben wrote neoclassic verse for the cultivated and aristocratic, Drayton aimed at a far wider reading public. Consequently, he insisted on printing his verse—"attempting," one recent critic persuasively argues, "to write for a national audience," not just for the Court or for Londoners but for an audience widely dispersed all through the country.[8] Although we assume the *Nymphidia* was written with an adult audience in mind, the calculated breadth of appeal for which Drayton strove certainly contributed to the comparative accessibility of his work to children. As a fairy story treated in the mock-heroic mode, the *Nymphidia* is constructed to give pleasure to various strata of the reading public—the well educated and the casual reader, the courtier-sophisticate and the country-traditionalist. The first two stanzas of *Nymphidia* announce Drayton's intention to cultivate this wide range of appeal:

> Olde CHAUCER doth of *Topas* tell
> Mad RABLAIS of *Pantagruell,*
> A latter third of *Dowsabell,*
>   with such poore trifles playing:
> Others the like have laboured at
> Some of this thing, and some of that,
> And many of they know not what,
>   But that they must be saying.
>
> Another sort there bee, that will
> Be talking of the Fayries still
> Nor never can they have their fill,
>   As they were wedded to them:
> No Tales of them their thirst can slake,
> So much delight therein they take,
> And some strange thing they faine would make,
>   Knew they the way to doe them.[9]

The first stanza announces the mock-heroic treatment of the subject, a technique specifically literary and presupposing the reader's familiarity with both ancient and modern classics of the heroic genre. Similarly, the range of allusion speaks to a well-educated audience, for Chaucer's English was rough going for many seventeenth-century readers and Rabelais was not widely available in English. But stanza two evokes the native, oral tradition of fairies—tricksters as familiar to children as to adults. Drayton then announces at the outset that he casts with a wide sweep, suggesting a readership of varied literary backgrounds and implicitly promising something for everyone, including young readers.

Among the pleasures to be shared by readers of every background, for example, are those imparted by meter, rhyme, and stanza form. It seems likely that a modern critic's observation that "poetry, unlike other forms of literature, is common ground for both children and grown-ups,"[10] would have been axiomatic in the early seventeenth century, when poetry still dominated prose as *the* medium of literary expression. *Nymphidia* is composed of eighty-eight verses of a surprisingly versatile eight-line stanza rhyming *aaabcccb*. It is a development of the six-line tail-rhyme stanza of Chaucer's *Sir Thopas* which was similarly designed to deflect the meter of the old heroic ballads and metrical romances to humorous purposes. Drayton's b-tail rhymes are double however and generally in trimeter as opposed to the tetrameter of the a- and c-lines. As one might expect, the effect of the short-line stanza built on triplets and punctuated with feminine rhymes is lively and mercurial. The poetic form complements the impetuous capering of the fairies and contributes significantly to the poem's sense of good fun. Drayton's absolute mastery of this frolicsome stanza is nowhere so evident as in the fairy Nymphidia's spell (409-32) in which the poet subdues his stanza for an incantation which might well have sent a pleasurable thrill through a young reader. A full appreciation of the comic effect of *Nymphidia's* stanza form finally depends upon reading the poem aloud so that the triplets and feminine rhymes may receive full emphasis.

Despite Drayton's references to Chaucer and Rabelais and his indebtedness to the stanza form of *Sir Thopas*, it is the fairy poetry of Shakespeare to which *Nymphidia* is most directly indebted. As numerous critics have pointed out, the domestic difficulties of Oberon and his queen in *A Midsummer Night's Dream* suggest the plot of *Nymphidia*, where in place of the changeling boy the complication is provided by a rival suitor for the Queen's favors.[11] The main plot—a court intrigue featuring the maneuvering and folly of Oberon, Queen Mab, and the rival suitor, the fairy-knight Pigwiggen—furnishes the focal action. Almost as important as the plot however are the minutely detailed descriptive passages, a *sine qua non* of fashionable post-Shakespearean fairy poetry (see Jonson, Herrick, William Browne), which derive from the famous description of Mab and her chariot in *Romeo and Juliet*. The whole occurs in an English pastoral setting with the actions of the principals treated in mock-heroic fashion, paralleling the antics of the tiny creatures with the heroes of classic and romance. Further, the sophisticated reader is invited to delight in the poet's and the fairies' blundering through such mock-epic conventions as the invocation to a muse; Oberon's heroic frenzy, mad as Ajax or Orlando Furioso; the inventory of the hero's armor; the formal preparations for a trial by combat; and the intervention of a goddess in the climactic combat.

It seems likely that a large segment of Drayton's intended audience, including most youthful readers, would not be able to appreciate fully the literary humor of much of this mock-heroic. For this less sophisticated audience, suggested by stanza two, Drayton offers pleasures of another kind. In addition to the broad-based appeal of the native fairy lore which Drayton generously loads into the interstices of the slender plot, the fairies' mock-heroic antics are genuinely humorous in their own right, without reference to literary models and allusions. The "minifying" technique,[12] popularized by Shakespeare's Queen Mab passage, results in descriptive passages of ingenuity and charm, and the English pastoral setting keeps the poem in contact with the contemporary countryside and its folklore. It is primarily these features of the *Nymphidia* which, once the poem was in the house, were capable of imparting a special kind of pleasure to children. Of course there is much in *Nymphidia*, as there is in *Gulliver's Travels*, which children will not understand, but Drayton has pitched his poem at such a broad audience that there is much more in the poem to which a child will respond with alacrity and delight.

The fairy folklore which informs *Nymphidia* draws directly on the familiar materials of childhood, the tales of fairies and sprites learned at mother's or nurse's knee and passed about from child to child. Thus, although Drayton's fairies may derive from a larger European tradition and may mock sophisticated codes of courtesy and conduct in their love and war, they are still, simultaneously, the fairies of the English countryside. Puck and Tom Thumb are here; the beauteous Queen Mab is still she of the Night-mare (53-56). The fairies engage in all the pursuits of traditional English fairy folklore—the pinching of mortals, the penny reward for cleanliness (65-68), the stealing of changelings (73-80). In combining the oral with the literary traditions of the fairy world, Drayton seeks to interest readers of every background, while incidentally providing for young readers a reassuringly familiar subject treated in a new way. Regardless of whether it was a part of Drayton's intent, in *Nymphidia* he created a bridge from the oral tradition of native folklore to the great world of European classical literature, a bridge most children of the time were constrained to cross in far more sober vehicles.

As the transition from one literary tradition to another might have challenged and excited the young reader of *Nymphidia*, so Drayton's descriptive technique, sharply detailed against the fantastic foreground, exerts a powerful imaginative appeal to the child in its equipoise of reality and fantasy. The stanzas describing the arming of the fairy knight Pigwiggen, who has challenged Oberon to combat, may serve as an example of this descriptive technique:

> And quickly Armes him for the Field,
> A little Cockle-shell his Shield,
> Which he could very bravely wield:
>   Yet could it not be pierced:
> His Speare a Bent both stiffe and strong,
> And well-neere of two Inches long;
> The Pyle was of a Horse-flyes tongue,
>   Whose sharpnesse naught reversed.
>
> And puts him on a coate of Male,
> Which was of a Fishes scale,
> That when his Foe should him assaile,
>   No poynt should be prevayling:
> His Rapier was a Hornets sting,
> It was a very dangerous thing:
> For if he chanc'd to hurt the King,
>   It would be long in healing.
>
>   [489-504]

Here the ingenuity of Drayton's description of his diminutive warrior equipped with rustic weapons and armor stimulates the imagination in the combination of the familiar and the fantastic. By carrying through this minifying technique—far more regularly than Shakespeare does in *A Midsummer Night's Dream*, though with less mathematical precision than Swift would employ in Lilliput—against the native pastoral background, Drayton goes far toward the creation of a self-contained universe of fairyland with an atmosphere and logic all its own. As in most successful fiction, this atmospheric unity derives largely from the key elements of the narrative: plot and character.

Despite rich descriptive passages and folklorist interpolations, *Nymphidia* possesses a clear plot furnished with plenty of action. Flirtatious Queen Mab is the central figure with Oberon and Pigwiggen, abetted by their agents Tom Thumb and Puck, in competition for her favor. The presumption of Mab's infidelity causes Oberon to run mad, after the fashion of Orlando Furioso. But in Drayton's miniaturized world, Oberon's frenzied encounters become increasingly farcical: he mistakes a glowworm for a devil, at a hive of bees he is thoroughly bedaubed with wax and honey, he tumbles off an ant he has mounted into more dirt and slime, he collides with a molehill which he takes for a mountain, he scales the molehill and falls down the other side into a lake. Oberon's mock-heroic misfortunes are harmless, simple and physical, of the pie-in-the-face variety which would delight a child who had never heard of Homer, Ariosto, or Cervantes. This plot pattern of sound and fury eventuating in laughter dominates the narrative, establishes the poem's tone, and dictates the happy ending, where Proserpina (no less) intervenes in the trial by combat between Oberon and Pigwiggen. "For feare lest they too much should bleed. / Which wondrously her troubled" (631-32), to set all right again through a judicious application of Lethe water. All exit "with mickle joy and merriment" (702), in harmony with the atmosphere of good humor which pervades the poem.

Within Drayton's miniature pastoral cosmos, the elphine protagonists mimic human passion and folly, thereby highlighting both the pettiness and the humor of aspects of the human condition customarily treated seriously. Here too there is an appeal to children who might not fully comprehend the intricacies of the love plot. In *Nymphidia*, the fairies behave like many human adults, controlled generally by passion and impulse rather than reason, averting tragedy as they carom around their picturesque universe only through luck or the fortuitous intervention of a providence they can't remember. And unlike the motivation of the fairies in *A Midsummer Night's Dream*, which is relatively complex, with multiple perspectives on most issues including the royal quarrel, *Nymphidia* simplifies and deemphasizes moral conflict by focusing on the ridiculous. Surely the spectacle presented by the fairies of adult posturing and folly in the name of love would delight all but the most unperceptive children.[13]

Nor is there a hidden moral lurking in the recesses of Drayton's fairy world to edify the unwary. The compulsive moralist might discern in the fairies' antics the old humanistic lesson of the folly and degradation of a life given over to blind passion. But if this is the message—and it seems criminal to abstract a moral so coldly from so lively and diaphanous a poem as this—it emerges only dimly and with difficulty.[14] Rather, the truth of the matter seems the obvious: *Nymphidia* is designed not to instruct but to delight by giving pleasure to different types of readers of widely diverse literary intelligence and comprehension.

In sum, *Nymphidia* possesses all the attributes of a successful fairy tale for children, even while it is demonstrably something other and more than that. It has fallen into neglect in our own time as the work of what one critic aptly calls "today the least fashionable of important Elizabethan poets."[15] If it is dismissed now as a narrative poem too long to fit comfortably into the standard anthologies of children's verse, it seems most unlikely *Nymphidia*'s rollicking good humor and capacity for imaginative stimulation would have escaped the notice of either Steele's friend Betty or the children of the preceding age. It is a work which deserves a prominent place not just in the annals of fairy poetry, but in the history of early English children's literature.

SEVEN

A Child's Garden of Sprites:
English Renaissance
Fairy Poetry

Ye elves of hills, brooks, standing lakes, and groves;
And ye, that on the sands with printless foot
Do chase the ebbing Neptune and do fly him
When he comes back; you demi-puppets that
By moonshine do the green sour ringlets make
Whereof the ewe not bites; and you, whose pastime
Is to make midnight mushrooms; that rejoice
To hear the solemn curfew. . .

The Tempest

Although the Elizabethan era, defined broadly as encompassing both the late sixteenth and early seventeenth centuries, has been aptly designated the "Golden Age" of English fairy poetry, it is well to recall that the poets of the period neither invented the fairies nor originated fairy poetry. As scholars and folklorists remind us, the fairies themselves have a rich history which extends in one direction back to the classical pantheons of Greece and Rome and in another deep

Bulletin of the West Virginia Association of College English Teachers 6 (1981): 37-54

into the roots of folk beliefs among the Celtic and Teutonic peoples who settled Great Britain.[1] And at various intervals, these creatures found their way into literature, into Gower and Chaucer and the "literary" tradition as well as the anonymous charms, ballads, and lyrics of the popular tradition. But only in the Elizabethan era did fairy poetry fire the imagination of the finest poets and appeal to a broad audience eager for news of the world of Faery. Setting aside Lord Berners' translation of *Huon of Bordeaux* (1534) which introduced Oberon to the English public, Edmund Spenser in his *Faerie Queene* (1590) first popularized fairies during the period with his accounts of the stirring deeds of elphine knights and ladies in a romantic fairyland inhabited by magicians, fays, monsters, and spirits of all sorts. Then in the mid-1590s, William Shakespeare utilized fairies as a major plot constituent of *A Midsummer Night's Dream* (performed c. 1595; printed 1600), transforming their traditional portrayal (one enthusiastic scholar even asserts Shakespeare "created a new supernaturalism" in his presentation of the fairies) and making them accessible to a wider and more representative audience. Shakespeare's portrayal of tiny creatures borne on gossamer wings proved so immediately popular that his conception became *the* literary image of fairies, inaugurating a flood of unabashedly imitative fairy poetry. During the first portion of the seventeenth century, poets of the stature of Jonson, Drayton, and Herrick joined with William Browne and other lesser talents to create a rich corpus of fairy poetry until, by mid-century, the fairy vogue ran its course. In this essay, I will survey some of the causes for the sudden popularity of fairy poetry in the English Renaissance and speculate on the staying power of the genre even while other Elizabethan fads, emblems, Petrarchan sonnets, epigrams, and such, ran their course and faded. Fairy poetry found a special niche in large part due to its appropriation by children, and the particular appeal of this poetry to Renaissance children is another area for exploration. Finally, through a survey of selected representative examples in different literary modes and times, I propose to study the development and direction of English fairy poetry during the period of its greatest prominence in English letters.

While the exact cause of fairy poetry popularity at the end of the sixteenth century is uncertain, there are many theories and a host of contributing factors. Minor W. Latham summarizes the speculations nicely in his *The Elizabethan Fairies*:

> There are a number of questions which occur to one's mind in regard to the prominence of the fairies during the 16th century in England. Did this vogue spring from a growing familiarity with the poems of Chaucer and Gower and with the medieval romances? Did an almost universal knowledge of classical mythology and a familiarity with the wood gods and spirits of Rome and Greece turn the literary man's thoughts to his own folklore? Was it the growing number of poets from the lower classes, fresh from the smaller villages and towns (where belief in the fairies was a matter of course), bound by no slavish adherence to authority nor limited by the dignity of scholarship, who put the fairies into poems and plays as naturally as had the classical poets, the nymphs and satyrs? The answers to these questions will always be conjectural.[2]

Clearly the ambiance, social and intellectual, of the late sixteenth century in England was a major factor in the literary exploitation of the fairies. Perhaps the decline in the belief in fairy magic and its role in the terrors of the night (a decline of belief which contrasts oddly with the new emphasis on rooting out witchcraft which King James brought to England) made of them fit ornaments for poetry. Or perhaps, as Latham suggests, the new yeoman class of poets, men like

Shakespeare and Drayton, brought with them the folklore of the villages and, in appealing to the burgeoning class of first-generation literates, turned to the familiar elves of the countryside for their supernatural machinery. In this regard, the great wave of English nationalism that marked the 1590s may also have been a contributing factor to the literary popularity of such indigenous sprites as Robin Goodfellow, alias Puck, who, like Queen Elizabeth herself, was "mere English." In any event, Shakespeare's assay into fairy poetry in *A Midsummer Night's Dream* demonstrated convincingly how ripe were the times for the fairy folk. Perhaps also the dynamic mix, sometimes almost a tension, of belief and disbelief in fairy magic stimulated the poets of the age, with credence widespread in the countryside though declining in the cities. Yet the seventeenth century is an age of infinite complexity and contradiction, and fairy belief may by no means be confined to the rural backwater. King James, no less, may stand witness to the complexity of attitude which characterized the age's fascination with the fairies. According to James in the *Demonology* he published in Scotland in 1597 and reprinted in London on his ascension in 1603, the world is overrun with devilish spirits seducing and plaguing honest folk, and the fourth class of spirits in James's enumeration are "the Phairie" with their king, queen, and train.[3] Yet James seems to have enjoyed fairy poetry, commended it in the court masques of Ben Jonson, and even, in Jonson's masque entitled *Oberon, The Faery Prince* (acted 1611; printed 1616), allowed his eldest son, Prince Henry, to act the titular part of the fairy prince. James's reaction had the Prince chosen to impersonate, say, the God of the Witches rather than the Prince of Fairies may be readily imagined; but regard for the fairy world, now hellish, now charming and whimsical, was obviously more complex, more ambivalent than popular attitudes toward other supernatural beings.

If the causes of the Elizabethan poets' new interest in the fairy world and the precise nature of the audience response are uncertain, there is no doubt of one fundamental: the popularity of fairy poetry. The literary appeal of fairies seems to cut right across class divisions. Shakespeare, popularizer and font of the Elizabethan literary fairies, brought them off the fringes of the plays of Lyly and Greene and set them at the center of *A Midsummer Night's Dream*, a play which depended for popularity upon pleasing a broad cross-section of Londoners; Ben Jonson, on the other hand, chiefly employed the fairy tribe in masques and aristocratic entertainments designed for the appreciation of an elite handful of participant-spectators; meanwhile Michael Drayton, one of the most accomplished and versatile of the Elizabethan journeymen poets, wrote of the fairies in order to sell books, recognizing and giving the broad book-buying public what it wanted, even as the balladmongers and booksellers poured out inexpensive collections for popular consumption like *Robin Goodfellow; His Mad Pranks, and Merry Jests* (1628). And as the fad of fairy poetry transcended classes in its appeal, even more naturally the literature of the fairies transcended distinctions of age, attracting children as readily as adults.

Speculation on the audiences of fairy poetry invariably leads to a discussion of the child as reader, since fairy stories and poems constitute a branch of literature children have always appropriated as their own. The key point to stress here is that in the Renaissance the choice is the child's rather than the author or bookseller's. With the exception of some schoolbooks, grammars, catechisms, and the like, children were not singled out for attention by the book trade as a special audience. Instead, Renaissance children were automatically part of the literary marketplace through such works as Aesop's *Fables*, a perennial favorite of all ages. Those authors, such as Shakespeare and Drayton, who sought a broad and representative public for their poetry thus wrote for a dual audience of adults and children. Therefore, there is little to be gained by seeking a special type of literature for entertainment targeted to the pre-adult population during our period; it does not exist. Yet children read, often voraciously, in the literature of the day, and for that reason a broad definition of a children's book, such as that promulgated by Sheila Egoff, is applicable: "In the true sense, a children's book is simply one in which a child finds pleasure."[4] Thus children read and thrilled to works such as John Foxe's great *Book of Martyrs* (1563), accessible in churches and public places all over England, which, in its combination of minute descriptions of hair-raising tortures with popular piety, the whole illustrated with graphic woodcuts of various tortures, could hardly have failed to rivet the attention of any but the most squeamish child. But children's preferred choice of reading matter was doubtless verse, for, as one modern critic has observed, "poetry, unlike other forms of literature, is common ground for both children and grown-ups."[5]

The fairies and their lore, done up into attractive verse and accompanied by an occasional woodcut, exerted a particular appeal to children which not even Foxe's horrific stories could rival. The adult world fed children's natural fascination with the magical and mysterious by positing a special connection between children and fairies centered upon the fairies' most notorious activity, the exchange of fairy offspring for human children. "The thing that everyone knows about the fairies," explains K.M. Briggs, "is that they covet human children and steal them whenever they can. No account of fairies is complete without the mention of this practice."[6] The timid child could experience a half-pleasurable thrill at the prospect of being kidnapped by marauding fairies, while the more adventurous youth could indulge secret dreams of

actually being a changeling, possessor of fairy powers un-
known and untapped, reservoirs of mystery and potency
foreign to both adults and peers. Certainly children who
were slightly built, dark-featured, or, most commonly, simply mischievous, must have been familiar enough with humorous adult exclamations about changelings to have set
them reflecting on the fairies. George Puttenham, while
defining a rhetorical trope in *The Arte of English Poesie* (1589),
gives us a glimpse of how common such humorous taunts
must have been in the mouths of nursemaids and those to
whom the care of children was entrusted:

The Greeks call this figure (*Hipallage*) the Latins *Submutatio*, we in
our vulgar may call him the (*vnderchange*) but I had rather haue him
called the (*Changeling*) nothing at all sweruing from his originall,
and much more aptly to the purpose, and pleasanter to beare in
memory: specially for you Ladies and pretie mistresses in Court,
for whose learning I write, because it is a terme often in their
mouthes, and alluding to the opinion of Nurses, who are want to
say, that the Fayries vse to steale the fairest children out of their
cradles, and put other ill fauoured in their places, which they called
changelings, or Elfs: so, if ye mark, doeth our Poet, or makes play
with his words, vsing a wrong construction for a right, and an
absurd for a sensible, by manner of exchange.[7]

The changeling swaps were but one of a host of fascinating
fairy activities familiar in the folklore of the countryside and
the villages. Children learned of their tricks, of the domestic
rituals through which the fairies might be propitiated, and of
the habits and character of Robin Goodfellow or Puck, the
most famous country spirit, from oral traditions and tales
before they began to read. Puck, especially, was a familiar
spirit to children and likely a convenient one also since all
manner of domestic mischances and accidents might be

blamed on him, for he was, as M.W. Latham notes, "the national practical joker" during our period.[8] And the fairy lore of the countryside (England was still predominantly rural country in the Renaissance) received concrete reinforcement from the fairy hills and dancing rings which dotted the countryside. A child could hardly escape the fairy presence, even should one wish to resist their allure. And a knowledge of the fairies and their ways could be a positive boon to a child, for the fairies were great gift-givers and he who was in the fairies' favor was fortunate indeed. Stories of fabulous fairy treasure buried in hills or left in bundles in the fields, by wells or pools, or the other places frequented by the creatures are legion. Meanwhile, the child who respected the fairies' regard for cleanliness and neatness and did his chores faithfully was often rewarded in the morning by a fairy gift of a six-pence in his shoes. In sum, the lore of the fairy world impinged at numerous points upon childhood and the folk tales of the tricks and doings of the fairies were an essential part of childhood during the English Renaissance.

Children thus imbibed a good deal of knowledge about fairies from their culture, including specifics about fairy activities which particularly involved children. Other causes for children's fascination with fairies may be adduced, such as their apparently instinctive affinity for the miniature, as in children's particular concern for puppies, kittens, birds, and the like. But it is most tempting to move beyond the social reference of this fairy lore to speculate upon the psychological attraction the world of fairy must have held for the Renaissance child. The fairies formed an invisible empire headquartered, according to popular opinion, underground inside the hills and caverns of the English countryside. They had a king and queen who presided over a state with laws and rules which not only fairies but mortals transgressed at their peril. The fairies thus constituted a kingdom within a kingdom, with alternate rules and life-styles altogether independent of the regulations and restrictions of the adult world familiar to children.

In fact, the fairy world, exalting mischief and the marvellous, often mocks the rules and values of the human adult world, with the characteristic activities of the fairies a burlesque of rational adult behavior. Against an adult world which constantly exhorted children, in church, school, and home, to grow up and adopt adult standards and values as rapidly as possible, the pastoral fairy world of escape and release stands as a striking antithesis, a realm of caprice and inversion, a subversive paradigm which must have delighted any child with spirit. And although diminutive in size, unlike real children the fairies were very potent through their possession of magical powers, enabling them to command propitiatory rites (the bowl of cream left on the doorstep overnight is one of the most familiar) from the adult population. As William Empson has observed in another context, "children like to think of being so small that they could hide from grown-ups and so big that they could control them."[9] In the fairies of Shakespeare and his followers, children have an alter ego which combines freedom from adult supervision with magical potency. And the fairies' occasional guerrilla raids on the adult model of ordered civilization make of them a literary rallying point for those such as pre-adults disenfranchised by their society.

Before leaving the rich topic of the psychological implications of children's fascination with fairyland, one final point of identification between the world of fairy and the psyche of the Renaissance child may be mentioned: the conception of time. As pastoral dwellers, probably descendents of agri-

cultural deities as the folklorists suggest, the fairies are re-
sponsive to the round of the seasons, but neither to larger nor
to more particular time frames. The fairies appear to lead a
kind of timeless existence, living for the day, oblivious to the
years, bound only by the seasonal cycle.[10] The similarity of
this time-consciousness to that characteristic of childhood is
striking; adults are bewildered by both. The stories of adults
who inadvertently or rashly blunder into a fairy ring or one of
the entrances of the fairies' underground kingdom and return
after what they believe to be a brief sojourn, of hours or days,
to find themselves years older illustrate this point. (Folklorists even trace the Rip Van Winkle story back to a fairy
archetype of this nature.)[11] From the stock of Renaissance
fairy beliefs, then, there seems ample evidence to support
the theory that the attraction of children for this body of
folklore, and its literary embodiment, works on several different levels, including a psychological appeal to a sense of
revolt, mischief, and freedom from adult supervision and
restraint.

The fountainhead of popular Renaissance fairy poetry is
Shakespeare's treatment of the fairies in *A Midsummer Night's
Dream*, a play probably performed only a short period after
Romeo and Juliet (1595). In a famous setpiece in the latter play,
Mercutio describes in exquisite detail Mab the Fairy Queen,
here presented as a miniature pastoral trickster. In *A Midsummer Night's Dream*, Shakespeare moves from description to
dramatic presentation of the silvan spirits, giving the entire
fairy troop a plot of their own as well as a primary role in the
denouement of the main plot. He develops the literary-
mythologic traditions of Oberon, "King of Shadows" Puck
calls him, and his queen, Titania, whose name suggests her
kinship with the classical pantheon, and mixes it with English
folk tradition of nature fairies, adding as a fillip to the mixture

the mischievous spirit Puck as Oberon's jester. The three separate classes of supernaturals represented by these diverse spirits have been admirably studied elsewhere as have the alterations in fairy lore Shakespeare made to suit his dramatic purposes.[12] He seems to have selected threads out of the skein of fairy beliefs and exaggerated them in such a manner as to produce a new conception made of familiar materials. The fairies are still mischievous, but no longer malicious, as they were so often in folk belief; where they had rewarded favored mortals with treasure, here they offer the benison of fairy magic on the union and house of their favorites; rather than being simply below normal human stature, they are miniaturized into tiny creatures (at least the fairy attendants are so); and their connection with the fields and woods is so emphasized as to make the fairies almost pastoral tutelary spirits. Indeed, almost every facet of Shakespeare's first indisputable comic masterpiece, including the fairies, has been subjected to extensive scholarly scrutiny; there yet remains, however, the consideration of the play's appeal to children.

Although the farcical staging of *Pyramus and Thisbe* by the artisans in Act V is a delight to audiences of all ages, the fairies must have been the center of interest for the children in Shakespeare's audience.[13] Here were the creatures familiar to them from ballad, nursery tale, and country lore trooping across the stage and leaving mischief and confusion in their wake. The fairy monarchs are squabbling upon their first entrance and, since Shakespeare presents them as elementals, their dispute has a direct impact on the country, which is buffeted by foul and unseasonable weather. The focal point of the quarrel between Oberon and Titania (and thus one of the hinges of the play's action since the human lovers' confusion in the central acts is a result of the fairy

quarrel) is a changeling boy which each wants. The changeling theme, often minimized or lost in scholarly discussions
of the play, would be of particular interest to the younger
members of the audience most liable to sudden "transporta-
tion," as Robin Starveling calls it in Act IV, by fairies. Shakespeare's treatment of the changeling theme in the play seems
specifically tailored to appeal to the imagination of a youthful
audience. Thus, the more frightening aspects of the changeling switch are discarded or suppressed while the adventurous potential is heightened. The child is not torn from its
human family, and there is no hint of forced abduction from
loved ones. Instead, the changeling boy is an orphan taken in
by Titania, who here seems less a goddess than a solicitous
maiden aunt. She dotes on the boy, setting her fairies to serve
him, and, according to Puck, she "Crowns him with flowers,
and makes him all her joy." The prospect of such an existence, with a lovely lady to entertain and play with one and
plenty of fairy servants to order about, must have had a good
deal of allure to the schoolboys, apprentices, and children
who found time from their chores to attend the play.

As soft and sybaritic as life as the apple of the Fairy
Queen's eye might be, however, Shakespeare presents the
changeling's alternative as better yet. Oberon wants the boy
to be his "henchman," a trusted knight in his wandering train
"to trace the forests wild." What adventurous lad would not
relish such an opportunity, especially after a diet of the soft
life in Titania's train. In *A Midsummer Night's Dream*, the human
boy enjoys serially both life-styles, thus providing an Elizabethan child a vicarious escape from tedium, chores, and
stern authority figures to a range of pleasures. Frequently in
performances of the play directors choose to put the changeling boy on stage in Act II as a member of Titania's train,
although he has no lines and is not listed among the *dramatis*

personae. Such an appearance usually intensifies the delight of children in the audience, as does the appearance of the sylvan fairies who attend on Oberon and Titania. Although we know too little of the original occasion and performance of the play, most scholars believe it was originally written on the occasion of a noble wedding, first performed at a great country house, and subsequently revised for the popular stage. C.L. Barber suggests that at the original performance "it seems quite possible that Peaseblossom, Cobweb, Moth, and Mustardseed were originally played by children of the family—their parts seem designed to be fool-proof for little children."[14] Whether or not this suggestion or some other, such as Ernest Schanzer's observation that Shakespeare may have had temporary access to the personnel of one of the boys companies to handle the fairy parts,[15] the roles of the fairies have always been performed by children, and the added attraction of seeing their peers impersonating fairy spirits must have drawn children to the theater.

Finally, Shakespeare's presentation of the fairies, which has been so widely hailed as popularizing the conception of fairies as tiny creatures, is hardly less important in solidifying and reinforcing the close connection between the fairies and the countryside, of "pastoralizing" the spirits. C.L. Barber writes perceptively of Shakespeare's emphasis on this aspect of fairy lore:

> His fairies are creatures of pastoral, varied by adapting folk superstitions so as to make a new sort of arcadia. Though they are not shepherds, they lead a life similarly occupied with the pleasures of song and dance and, for king and queen, the vexations and pleasures of love. They have not the pastoral "labours" of tending flocks, but equivalent duties are suggested in the tending of nature's fragile beauties, killing "cankers in the muskrose buds." They have a freedom like that of shepherds in arcadias, but raised to a higher

power: they are free not only of the limitations of place and purse but of space and time.[16]

Fairies are country spirits, alien to the city and to many urban values, and they enter the city rarely and with reluctance; usually, to traffic with the fairies, one must go to the countryside, their domain. When they do pay these infrequent visits, as at Midsummer or Halloween, to exchange a child or bless a favorite mortal, mischief and confusion often attend them, even when their intent, as in *A Midsummer Night's Dream*, is good. This seems to be the case because the fairies represent an ethic foreign to that of daylight urban society (theirs is "the night rule" as Puck calls it) and when the two collide, confusion is an inevitable consequence. Although the appeal of the fairy ethic to an audience of children has been discussed, it is also necessary to notice the formal function of the fairy ethic, especially as it resembles the model of the traditional literary pastoral. Barber notes many of the obvious pastoral trappings of Shakespeare's fairies, but he does not press the functional similarity between the fairy ethic and activity and that of the literary pastoral. The pastoral in the Renaissance presents an alternate life-style in contrast to urban existence, and it is inherently a criticism of urban values.[17] Fairyland often borrows the trappings of pastoral not only on its surface but in its function; it too amuses and instructs to life by proposing an alternate life-style and value system by which quotidian existence may be measured, judged, and, ideally, improved. Of course, the fairy frolic, like the sedentary shepherd's life in the literary pastoral, is not intended as a literal or practicable alternative to maturity and civilization; neither is ideal. Like the pastoral and the state of childhood itself, however, fairyland manifests customs, values, and behavior alien to adult urban culture, and yet all these variant life-styles, whatever the manner of their metaphoric presentation, can teach important lessons about the values of play, release, harmony, and the natural life. And like the pastoral, the fairy culture of the countryside affords a detached vantage point for studying adult civilization where, as Puck truly sees, "Lord, what fools these mortals be."

Within *A Midsummer Night's Dream*, the spokesman for much of the good-humored criticism of adult values and activities is Puck or Robin Goodfellow. Although Shakespeare makes him a fairy spirit of one sort or another to serve as Oberon's jester, he was best known to every child as Puck, Pook, or Pug, a mischievous goblin whose tricks were familiar to every country household.[18] Indeed, Puck was so well known to English audiences and his critiques of humanity so popular that in 1604 Shakespeare's play was actually performed at court under the title *A Play of Robin Goodfellow*. As a country spirit familiar to all, the prankster is a comfortable reference point for children unfamiliar with Titania and such fairies as derive from literary tradition. Thus children reading or seeing the play (and as popular drama *A Midsummer Night's Dream* is accessible to both the illiterate and pre-literate such as small children) may enjoy a double pleasure in Shakespeare's fairies; they are treated to the pleasant and familiar tricks of Puck (enumerated at 2.1.34-54), building on such fairy lore as they bring to the theater with them, while broadening their knowledge of the spirits through acquaintance with Titania and Oberon. The eclectic nature of the fairy lore used by Shakespeare, Drayton, and the poets of the age is the despair of many critics, who assume a confusion in the mind of the poets as the source of the odd amalgam of classical, literary, native, and made-up spirit lore in such plays as *A Midsummer Night's Dream*. It seems at least as plausi-

ble, however, to see the mixture of satyrs, sylphs, hobgob-
lins, and elves in this poetry as a conscious attempt to reach
and entertain the broadest possible audience, including children, by domesticating classical spirits and elevating native
country fairies to compete with ancient and foreign spirits.

The same mixture of native and foreign, ancient and
contemporary spirits is seen throughout the work of Ben
Jonson, who prided himself on his classical learning. Jonson
wrote poems, entertainments, masques, and plays featuring
the fairy tribe. One of his earliest fairy pieces, entitled *The
Entertainment at Althrope* or *The Satyr*, is of particular interest
because it was written for a child, Prince Henry, age nine,
who takes a part in the entertainment. The entertainment
was commissioned by Sir Robert Spencer on the occasion of
the visit to Althrope by the new Queen and Prince upon their
first coming into England in 1603 to join King James. The
plot is typically slender: Puck (identified in the tags as
"Satyr," although called "Pug" by the elves and identified
from the account of his activities as Robin Goodfellow) meets
Mab the Fairy Queen and her fairies; they have a quarrel
which results in Puck being pinched into submission; and
their rivalry is subordinated so they may do homage to the
Queen and Prince, who are also presented by the fairies with
a precious jewel.

Jonson's choice of fairies as subject matter for his first
presentation before the royal family, at a time when all the
English poets were rushing to curry favor with the House of
Stuart, deserves consideration. First, the entertainment
would surely please the young prince and heir apparent, for
the fascination of children with fairies seems universal and is
irrespective of national borders. Jonson's success in his selection of subject may be gauged by the fact that eight years
later, on the occasion of the formal investiture of Henry as

Prince of Wales, Jonson wrote a masque, *Oberon, The Faery Prince: A Masque of Prince Henries*, in which the Prince, now a teenager, took the titular role. Also, the time was appropriate, for the Queen and Prince were scheduled to arrive at Althrope on Midsummer Day, a traditional time of fairy magic. The choice of English fairies to greet the Scottish queen and prince also conveys a practical political statement. They are native spirits, mischievous and lively, as apt to quarrel among themselves as are Englishmen. Although Pug is struck with instinctive admiration for the Queen and Prince, this does not stop him from getting into a quarrel with Mab, who has come to welcome and bless the new rulers. Pug is punished for his obstinancy in the traditional fairy manner, being pinched black and blue by Mab's elves, and all the fairies unite to bless the royal house and convey the jewel to the Queen.[19] Thus the English people, ever xenophobic and as naturally restless as the fairies, may be inclined to potential mischief, but they require only the strong hand and right order of the House of Stuart to call forth the admiration and obedience instinct within them. The entertainment thus serves the masque function of illustrating the manner in which discordant elements—here represented by Pug and, to a lesser extent, the other fairies—may be naturally subordinated to and controlled by their superiors, in the person of royalty, in an affirmation of the status quo. Mab's welcoming speech to the Queen makes this subordination of discord to right order clear:

> Pardon lady this wild strayne,
> Common with the SYLVAN trayne,
> That doe skip about this plaine:
> *Elues*, apply your gyre againe.
>
> And whilst some doe hop the ring.
> Some shall play, and some shall sing,

Wee'le expresse in euery thing,
OR (I)ANAS well-comming.[20]

Thus the *Entertainment at Althrope*, like *A Midsummer Night's Dream*, was intended to be appreciated on different levels; the young prince would have enjoyed the fairies and their frolic, while his mother would have understood and appreciated the political compliment conveyed through the English fairies scarcely less than the jewel bestowed upon her. For Henry and the children of the house, in particular, the rich mixture of fairy frolic and fairy lore must have been irresistible. The fairy dancers first appear dancing in "an artificiall ring" around Mab and later do "a fantastique dance"; their antics then extend to hopping about the "cream-bowle," Mab's nocturnal raids on the dairy, where she can "hurt; or helpe the cherning," pinching country wenches for punishment, leaving testers (sixpence) in their shoes if favorably disposed toward them, and include such fairy magic as a curious account of the changeling transaction: "This is shee, that empties cradles, / Takes out children, puts in ladles." The work was evidently popular, as indicated by a separate quarto publication in 1604 as well as inclusion by Jonson in the folio edition of his works in 1616.

Much more popular than Jonson's *Entertainment* or various fairy pieces was Michael Drayton's *Nymphidia, The Court of Fayrie* (1627), a narrative poem discussed in the preceding chapter. As with the fairy pieces of Shakespeare and Jonson discussed above, *Nymphidia* appeals on several levels to the diverse elements of Drayton's audience, and to reach this audience, he too combines literary with oral traditions of fairy lore.

There is much to amuse a child in the eighty-eight stanzas of rollicking verse which set forth the mishaps, confusion, and happy conclusion of this farcical tale of love and chivalry in fairyland. Although Drayton's treatment of his fairy story is relatively sophisticated, a mock-heroic burlesque of the *chansons de gestes* materials familiar through the romances of Mallory, Ariosto, Spenser, and others, the plot line is clear and straightforward, the characters simple and vivid, and the whole work thus accessible to audiences unfamiliar with the specific literary works and chivalric conventions being burlesqued. To a child, the humor in such mishaps as Oberon's tumble down the molehill is straightforward, physical, and spontaneous, akin to the modern child's delight at Wylie Coyote's Saturday morning misfortunes in pursuit of the Roadrunner.

The fairy plot of *Nymphidia* is not interwoven with several other plots, as is the case in *A Midsummer Night's Dream*, nor is it bent to didactic or epideictic ends, as in Jonson's entertainment. Drayton's poem gains in focus, concentration, and unity of atmosphere to create a self-contained universe of fairyland in which a child may lose himself. To achieve this effect, Drayton makes maximum use of the "minifying" technique[21] popularized by Shakespeare's Queen Mab passage in *Romeo and Juliet*, providing extensive descriptive passages of ingenuity and charm rooted firmly in the real English countryside. Here the blend of the familiar materials of the countryside, minutely detailed, with the fantastic miniaturization of the fairies, exerts a powerful imaginative appeal to the child in its equipoise of reality and fantasy, as in the stanzas describing the arming of the fairy knight Pigwiggen for his combat with Oberon:

> And quickly Armes him for the Field,
> A little cockle-shell his Shield,
> Which he could very bravely wield:

> Yet could it not be pierced:
> His Speare a Bent both stiffe and strong,
> And well-neere of two Inches long:
> The Pyle was of a Horse-flyes tongue,
>   Whose sharpnesse naught reversed.
>
> And puts him on a coate of Male,
> Which was of a Fishes scale,
> That when his Foe should him assaile,
> No poynt should be prevayling:
> His Rapier was a Hornets sting,
> It was a very dangerous thing:
> For if he chanc'd to hurt the King,'
>   It would be long in healing.[22]

Such passages, mixing the familiar and fantastic in a display
of poetic virtuosity, are a primary source of pleasure in the
poem, uniting with a strong plot and vivid characterization
to shape an eminently successful fairy tale for children.

As fine a fairy poem as *Nymphidia* is, however, the seeds of
decadence are evident in its texture. The relevance of the
fairies and their antics to the real world of human beings is
less clear than in Shakespeare or Jonson and the descriptive
passages bulk larger and contribute more to the success of the
poem than in the earlier poets' fairy verse. In a curious little
anthology of fairy poetry entitled *A Description Of the King and
Queene of Fayries, their habit, fare, their abode, pompe, and state*
(1635), compiled by one "R.S.," the tendencies toward simple literary escapism and ingenious prettification may be
observed writ large.[23] This brief collection (five poems in
twenty-two duodecimo pages, including three blank and four
with woodcuts) begins with a poem entitled "A Description
of the King of *Fayries* Clothes, brought to him on New-yeares
day in the morning, 1626, by his Queenes Chambermaids."
Although R.S. prints it as an anonymous forty-four line

poem, in other seventeenth century manuscripts it is clear
that the complete poem is actually seventy-six lines long and
the work of Sir Simeon Stewart, a friend of Robert Herrick's.
A brief selection of one of the stanzas from Stewart's poem
will illustrate its flavor:

> A rich Wastcoat they did bring,
> Made of the Trout-flies gilded wing;
> At which his Elveship gan to fret,
> Swearing it would make him sweat
> Even with it weight: he neede would weare
> A wascoat made of downy hare,
> New shaven of an Eunuchs chin,
> That pleas'd him well, t'was wondrous thin.[24]

The poem is, as the title suggests, a static pastoral blazon,
a listing of the fairy king's wardrobe and accouterments.
There is no plot, character development, or significance of
any kind to the poem. Instead the fairy monarch is a peg on
which the poet can hang the most elaborate and ingenious
conceits he can work, such as the conceit of the eunuch's
beard which is to serve for Oberon's waistcoat. Unfortunately, Stewart's poem does not represent an aberration or a
genuine failure of poetic talent or inspiration; rather, it is
representative of the level to which fairy poetry had sunk as
the century wore on. For evidence of this decline, the next
poem in the anthology, "A Description of his Dyet," may be
adduced. The poem is, in fact, an abbreviated early version
of "Oberon's Feast" by Robert Herrick, printed in full in his
Hesperides (1648). Although a gifted poet, hailed by Edmund
Gosse as "the last laureate of Fairyland,"[27] Herrick here, as in
much of his other fairy poetry, is too often content with the
static, clever, and cute. Thus, as in the following passage, the
poem rattles along with a list of the miniature pastoral
comestibles fit for the fairy king:

> Moles eyes he tastes, the Adders eares;
> To these for sauce the slaine stagges teares
> A bloted earewig, and the pith
> Of sugred rush he glads him with.[26]

The spectacle of the fairy king munching on snake's ears is, unfortunately, a portent of what is to follow until he polishes off his meal with "silke wormes sperme" and a concoction of "the blood of fleas / Which gave his Elveships stomache ease." Indeed, the only poem in the fairy anthology which escapes the pervading desire for a prettiness bred of ingenious minification oblivious to the world of humanity and its concerns is an anonymous lyric entitled "The Fairies Fegaries." It is a song in eight stanzas sung by the fairy queen to her elves detailing the activities and sports of her tribe:

> Come follow, follow me,
> You Fairie Elves that be:
> And circle round this greene,
> Come follow me your Queene.
> Hand in hand lets dance a round,
> For this place is Fayrie ground.
>
> When mortals are at rest,
> And snorting in their nest,
> Unheard, or unespy'd
> Through key-holes we do glide:
> Over tables, stooles and shelves,
> We trip it with our Fairie Elves.
>
> And if the house be foule,
> Or platter, dish, or bowle,
> Upstairs we nimbly creepe,
> And finde the sluts asleepe:
> Then we pinch their armes and thighes,
> None escapes, nor none espies.

But if the house be swept,
And from uncleannesse kept,
We praise the house and maid,
And surely she is paid:
For we do use before we go
To drop a Tester in her shoe.

Upon the mushrooms head,
Our table cloth we spread
A graine o' th' finest wheat
Is manchet that we eate:
The pearlie drops of dew we drinke
In Akorne-cups fill'd to the brinke.[27]

Although a lyric, the poem has a firm shape and movement in describing fairy activity. It avoids the imagistic excesses that make the other poems in the anthology so often seem merely precious. In particular, the account of fairy activities, especially the raids on mortals and the fairy frolics in the fields, reflect and build on the folklore familiar to children of the age. But "The Fairies Fegaries" is an exception to the general tenor of late Jacobean fairy poetry represented in this collection; the bulk of the collection reflects a fatal obsession with minification for its own sake, a cloying prettiness, and an empty triviality. It is little wonder the better poets soon abandoned the fairies as suitable subjects for serious poetry and the general public consigned such verse to the nursery, fit only for what was construed as the simple tastes of children.

This survey of the rise and decline of fairy poetry in the English Renaissance suggests several fruitful avenues for further study. The relationship of the literary pastoral and fairy poetry, for example, seems indisputable, but the effect of the pastoral influence is questionable. The pastoralization process tends to emasculate and trivialize the fairies; paradoxically, the more closely they are tied to the countryside the tighter the poets' focus on minute details of the fairies' pastoral equipage and activities and the farther the fairy world is removed from the serious function of pastoral to offer a criticism of life. The contrast between fairy ways and human ones, explicit in Shakespeare and Jonson and clearly implicit in Drayton, disappears by the time of Herrick, the Dutchess of Newcastle, and the later seventeenth-century fairy poets. Minification, one technique in the presentation of Shakespeare's fairies, becomes a self-sufficient end in itself and the pastoral sphere of fairy activity becomes increasingly isolated, until fairyland ceases to have any real relevance or relationship to the world of human beings. Fairy poetry becomes static, tedious, and irrelevant. Thus, as Delattre laments, fairy poetry "may be said to be extinct in England about 1650."[28]

The poets' loss of interest in the fairies as a vehicle for psychological release, social commentary, or poetic significance is at least as important to the death of fairy poetry in the seventeenth century as the putative general decline of belief in the fairy world. The poets of mid-century, Vaughan, Lovelace, Marvell, Denham, and others, revived and reworked the pastoral tradition in many interesting ways, but they did not utilize the fairies, whose literary escapades had come to seem less fit for the consumption of a broad reading public than as toys and trifles fit only to amuse children. Nevertheless, the post-Renaissance construction in the scope, aims, and target audience of English fairy poetry should not be allowed to obscure the achievement of the Elizabethan laureates of the little folk. In their poetry, adults no less than children could find delight and release in an imaginative fairy world which retained its relevance to the human world.

EIGHT

The Water-Poet:
A Pioneer of Children's
Literature

The genres identified by the eighteenth and nineteenth centuries as particularly appropriate for children's reading grew from the fertile soil of the English Renaissance. It is true that much of the literature written exclusively for children during the earlier period is so didactic and dreary that at best it seems only a faint harbinger of Newbery and the profusion of Victorian children's books. Instead of focusing too narrowly on these didactic works for evidence of the development of distinctive genres in English children's literature, however, the researcher investigating the historical roots of children's literature needs to look back to the works written for a general audience of readers during the Renaissance, books and pamphlets whose appeal was inclusive and eclectic. Thus, for example, students of the period have been long aware that the chapbook versions of the old medieval romances published during the late sixteenth and early seventeenth centuries for a general audience exerted a strong appeal to young readers and may be considered early anticipations of such works as Thomas Boreman's *Gigantic Histories* in the eighteenth century and the Victorian treatment of Robin Hood or King Arthur and his knights in children's versions.

This study intends to resurrect a generally forgotten early seventeenth century author who pioneered in publishing several distinct types of literature which, like the simplified adventure stories of the chapbooks, subsequent generations identified as peculiarly suitable for and appealing to children. The author is John Taylor, known in his own day as the Water-Poet, who during his long life from 1580 to 1653 established himself as one of the most prolific popular writers of the English Renaissance.[1] After a leg injury brought his career as a waterman to a halt around 1600, Taylor began writing pamphlets, in verse and prose, on all manner of subjects and he managed for the next half-century to support himself by his pen. Taylor poured out a torrent of variegated popular works, such as a biography of the Virgin Mary, elegies on public figures (written to order at incredible speed), satires and miscellanies, popular and novelty editions of standard works, pastorals, guidebooks, assorted items of popular journalism, including a praise of clean linen, a description of British ales, and accounts of the oldest man and of the biggest eater in England.

In his continual scrambling to catch the ear of the popular audience, Taylor initiated in England several types of literature which are considered today as important genres within the corpus of children's literature. He was the first to introduce to the English reading public simplified miniature redactions of the Bible, nonsense verse, and the animal story of the noble pet aiding and succouring his master. In inexpensive editions often published by Taylor himself and hawked by both the author and the booksellers around St. Paul's, Taylor's books were the common property of adults and children; but within another century, these distinctive literary types and forms pioneered by Taylor—"thumb Bibles," nonsense verse, and animal stories—were relegated by the adult reading public to the nursery, where their progeny thrived, delighting generations of young readers. An examination of the constituents of these three juvenile literary forms at the point where they first came into English must begin with a consideration of the readership of the chapbook literature of the early seventeenth century.

The entire question of the readership of the cheap books (hence, "chapbooks") and pamphlets that poured from the presses of Renaissance England is described in the most recent study of the subject as "maddeningly obscure."[2] The late sixteenth century was a dynamic period in which social, technological, and educational changes of great significance for the English publishing industry occurred. Of particular interest is the dramatic rise in the number and type of readers during the period, their enormous and catholic appetite for inexpensive reading matter, and the emergence of both a group of authors eager to write for the popular market and a proliferation of publishers and booksellers prepared to handle such productions. Louis Wright and H.S. Bennett, in particular, have explored the ramifications of the rapid growth of endowed grammar schools in the sixteenth century, a phenomenon that contributed to increased childhood literacy in the period.[3] More recent research, however, suggests that the acquisition of reading skills by Renaissance children was far more common than previously believed. Margaret Spufford, for example, has convincingly argued the unreliability of the historians' traditional test of literacy during the period: the ability to sign one's name.[4] As she points out, because reading was commonly taught in the grammar schools a year before writing, many less advantaged boys who entered the work force at the traditional age of seven had learned to read but not to write, a skill customarily taught in the schools to eight-year-olds. And although girls were not taught to write as a matter of course until the end of the eighteenth century, they were often taught to read; indeed, in strong Protestant and Puritan households, evidence suggests they were expected to be able to read in order to help guide their families in godly paths.[5] Puritanism especially laid heavy stress on the necessity for each individual, male or female, to read and study the Bible for himself.

The rapid spread of literacy down from aristocratic circles through the ranks of English society helped create a broad popular market for journalistic pamphlets of every sort, and by the 1590s professional writers such as Robert Greene, Thomas Deloney, Thomas Heywood, and others were able to support themselves by writing to this market. Among this group John Taylor is one of the most interesting because of his entrepreneurial skill and the breadth of his indefatigable experimentation in a variety of popular literary forms. Taylor tried his hand at anything that might find a popular audience. In the process, he learned it was possible to make a profit by writing for a relatively narrow, specialized audience, as in his several tracts on behalf of his old company, the London watermen. And while churning out elegies, cookbooks, satires, and all sorts of items of popular journalism, Taylor also experimented with various methods of bringing his productions to the largest possible audience. For example, he wrote a number of travel pamphlets detailing journeys he had undertaken around England which he sold on a subscription basis.[6] Taylor would post advertisements (called "Taylor's bills") in pubs and other public places announcing a forthcoming trip and inviting people to sign their names to the bills as an informal promise to purchase a copy of Taylor's account of his trip upon his successful return. Armed with a list of subscribers, Taylor would then contract directly with a printer for however many copies he thought he could sell on consignment through the booksellers' stalls and country chapmen as well as through his own direct sales. No one in England had attempted subscription publishing on this scale before,[7] and Taylor's success with this strategem enabled him to bypass the Stationers' Company and to order printings of his works far in excess of the normal 1500-copy press runs.[8] Such entrepreneurial activities, which helped break the Stationers' Company monopoly on London printing, earn Taylor a place in most histories of printing in England.[9]

Thus, Taylor was an innovative, ever commercial writer, customarily aiming at a broad, inclusive audience but willing to experiment with specialty items and publications designed for more limited circulation. In brief, he is the sort of popular author who might have targeted specifically the growing audience of young readers in the early seventeenth century. The exact date at which children were recognized by authors and publishers as a viable target audience for nondidactic works is very difficult to define with precision. Most recently, B.A. Brockman has demonstrated how the Robin Hood chapbooks of the century were increasingly aimed at and considered to be the property of an audience of children.[10] And Margaret Spufford's analysis of the impact of the youthful audience on the publishing scene by the Restoration leads her to conclude that "schoolboys do not immediately leap to mind as a market worth publishing for, but the chapbook publishers thought otherwise."[11] Children and apprentices mingled with other browsers among the open bookstalls of Paul's Walk and, with a range of broadsides and chapbooks priced at a penny or two, youth composed a significant potential market.[12] Even out in the country towns, itinerant chapmen and peddlers like Shakespeare's Autolycus made it possible for even a poor boy like John Bunyan to have access to the blood-and-thunder tales of Sir

Bevis of Southampton and St. George. Thus, the seventeenth century witnessed the increasing identification of chapbook culture with a juvenile audience, especially in such distinct forms as the adventure story.

An assessment of John Taylor's contribution to the emergence of distinct genres of children's literature focuses upon three chapbooks he published relatively early in his career, when he was exploring the reading public for receptive audiences. For the first few years following his literary debut with *The Sculler . . . or Gallimawfry of Sonnets, Satyres, and Epigrams* (1612), Taylor probed the tastes of the reading public with a mix of chapbooks, serious or merry, in verse or in prose.[13] In 1614 he brought out in two parts a tiny book, approximately 1⅛" X 1¼", containing a versified synopsis of the Old and New Testaments and Apocrypha. The Old Testament volume, entitled *Verbum Sempiternae* (corrected in 1616 and later editions to *Sempiternum*; Taylor frequently apologizes in his works for his slender grasp of the classical languages), and the New Testament one, *Salvator Mundi*, were bound separately in this original edition, but thereafter they were bound together, often in dos-á-dos fashion. This publication is a good example of Taylor's strengths, which always lay less in his modest literary talent than in his marketing skills: his ability to spot or even to create a literary trend, to identify the optimum readership group for a work, and to devise an appropriate delivery system for packaging and getting the work to its proper audience. Taylor invented neither the versified Bible synopsis nor the miniature book. Instead, he recognized the popular potential appeal of such works as Henoch Clapham's ponderous *A Briefe Of the Bible, Drawne First into English Poesy, and then illustrated by apte Annotations* (1596) and the attractive packaging of John Weever's diminutive 1½" X 1⅛" *An Agnus Dei* (1601), a volume containing a rhymed life of Christ. Drawing on both examples, Taylor created the first English "thumb Bible" (the term itself seems to be a Victorian one).[14] At least seven editions of the book appeared in the seventeenth century and perhaps a hundred editions of Taylor's text, often without acknowledgment of his authorship, were published by the end of the nineteenth century in small volumes intended for children.

Although historically Taylor is unquestionably the originator and popularizer of the thumb Bible and progenitor of all the miniature decorated children's Bibles of the eighteenth and nineteenth centuries, the question of Taylor's original target audience remains. The issue is important because some students of the field will allow the classification of children's literature to apply only to those works of "imaginative literature marketed to children and designed for their amusement as well as edification";[15] others, of course, elect a less restrictive, more comprehensive definition, ranging all the way up to Sheila Egoff's claim that a children's book is any book that gives pleasure to children.[16] Taylor does not directly identify his target audience of the *Verbum*; given the eagerness of the Renaissance public for religious, and especially biblical, knowledge, Taylor no doubt thought his book appropriate for all audiences. Still, evidence of various sorts suggests the special appeal of the book to a youthful audience.

Most obviously, the physical size of Taylor's book suggests an appeal to children. As Abraham S.W. Rosenbach observes, "Printers early discovered that books for children should be made in proportion to their little clients—small. Miniature volumes have always had a great fascination for children of all ages. Their very neatness and compactness make them seem the more precious and desirable."[17] Taylor's little volume would fit neatly into a small palm or pocket, and, as Ruth MacDonald notes, with a single couplet of verse on each page, "reading and turning pages gives a certain pleasant rhythm to the book."[18] If the book were particularly pleasing physically to children, it appears also to have been priced within the means of pious or indulgent parents—or, indeed, of the children themselves. Most of Taylor's chapbook publications were designed to sell for less than sixpence; although the price of the miniature *Verbum* is only conjectural, Taylor makes a point of stressing its inexpensiveness in his introduction of *Salvator Mundi*, dedicated to Prince Charles:

> To the Reader
> Here, Reader, maist thou read (for little cost)
> How thou wast ransom'd, when thou quite wast lost.[19]

And the content would have been no less entertaining than useful to young readers. Taylor was always more of a rhymester than a poet, and his facile couplets summarizing the books of the Bible display his talents to advantage. Both verse and rhyme would appeal to a juvenile audience, while the utility of the *Verbum* is obvious. "Certainly," as Ruth MacDonald observes, "this book might have served as an excellent memory device for children trying to remember the books of the Bible and their contents."[20] Finally, there is a rare piece of evidence that Taylor's versified Bible synopsis was given to children in the early seventeenth century. Ruth E. Adomeit reports the existence in the Houghton Library at Harvard University of an "unique handwritten copy of the Taylor *Verbum Sempiternum*. Less than 2 inches tall in a green silk dos-á-dos binding, it was written in 1615 by Esther Inglis, the famous calligrapher, for her son, Samuel Kello."[21] And despite the popularity of the thumb Bible, like the popular chapbook romances which were anathematized by educators as trivializations of their texts and contributions to youth's waywardness, Taylor's *Verbum* was included in blasts emanating from the conservative establishment at popularizers who rhyme the Bible.[22] Typically, Taylor was undeterred by criticism and, in fact, he went on to publish, in 1617, a tiny verse abridgment, about 1½" X 1", of John Foxe's classic *Book of Martyrs*. The format, with a single distich on each page, is similar to that of the *Verbum*, but Taylor's Foxe volume seems to have been less successful than his earlier venture, and he attempted no more miniature abridgments.[23]

Another of Taylor's early productions also stands near the beginning of a type of children's literature perfected only in the nineteenth century: nonsense verse. Nursery rhymes and nonsense songs are to be found throughout the Renaissance period, but sustained and self-contained works of narrative verse in a pure nonsense mode are very rare prior to the advent of Lear's Jumblies and Carroll's Snark in the Victorian age. Taylor's entry in the field of nonsense verse, published in 1622—although, as a part of the fooling, the title page sports the futuristic date of 1700—is entitled *Sir Gregory Nonsence His Newes from no place. Written on purpose, with much study to no end, plentifully stored with want of wit, learning, Iudgement, Rime and Reason, and may seeme very fitly for the understanding of Nobody*. This piece is so curious and, unlike the *Verbum*, so little known, that a description of it is required to indicate its central features and nonsense characteristics.

Taylor begins with a double dedication of his work. First, in acknowledgment of the popular body of nonsense tales gathered around the mad men of Gotham, he dedicates it to "Master Trim Tram Senceles of the famous City of Goteham" and also to Nobody. Next comes a prose proem to frame Sir Gregory's news. A sample of Taylor's prose from this section will illustrate his characteristic method:

Vpon a Christmas Euen, somewhat night (sic) Easter, anon after Whitsuntide, walking in a coach from London to Lambeth by

water, I ouertooke a man that met me in the morning before sunne
set, the wind being in *Capricorne*, the Signe *Southwest*, with silence I
demanded many questions of him, and hee with much pensiuenesse
did answere me merrily to the full, with such ample and empty
replications, that both our understandings being equally satisfied,
we contentiously agreed to finish and prosecute the narration of
the unknowne Knight Sir *Gregory Nonsence*, so sitting down upon our
shoulders, resting uneasily on a banke of Sicamores under a Tree of
odoriferous and contagious Camomile, after three sighs, smilingly
uttered in the Hebrew Character, two grones from the Chaldean
Dialect, five sobs from the Arabian Sinquapace, sixe dumps from
Germane Idiome, nine Moodes of Melancholly from the Italian
tongue, with one hub hub from the Hiberbian outcry. And last he
laughed in the Cambrian tongue, and beganne to declare in the
Vtopian speech, what I haue heare with most diligent negligence
translated into the English Language, in which if the Printer hath
placed any line, letter or sillable, whereby this large volume may
bee made guilty to bee vnderstood by any man, I would haue the
Reader not to impute the fault to the Author, for it was farre from
his purpose to write to any purpose, so ending at the beginning, I
saw as it is applawsfully written and commended to posterity in the
Midsommer nights dreame. If we offend, it is with our good will,
we came with no intent, but to offend, and shew our simple skill.[24]

Taylor's inspiration for Sir Gregory Nonsence and his tale
is thus not only folk humor and popular jokes about the mad
Gothamites but also the burlesque antics of Bottom and his
mates in their performance of *Pyramus and Thisbe*. The
egregious folly of the mad men of Gotham is echoed in
Taylor's string of impossible contradictions, while his attempt
to turn the language as well as the sense inside out evidently
derives from the linguistic chaos of Shakespeare's artisans'
encounter with classical tragedy. The proem is succeeded by
a table of "The names of such Authors Alphabetically recited
as are simply mentioned in this Worke" (Sig. [A5]), a list

which runs from Amadis de Gaul to Zany on tumbling, including Jack Drum, Long Meg, *A Hundred Merry Tales*, Tarleton, Tom Thumb, Bevis of Southampton, and the Dunsmore Cow. Of course, most of these worthies are not, in fact, cited in the work at all, but they suggest the rich texture of jestbooks, chapbook romances, and popular entertainments which made up the popular culture of Renaissance England. In a similar fashion, Taylor includes a page of "Faults escaped in the Printing, which a wise reader may mend when he sees them." Of course, Taylor expects no wise readers, which is just as well since his list features topsy-turvy changes on pages that don't exist in the chapbook (*e.g.*, "In the 37. page, and 1. line, for *vice* read *plenty.*/ In the ooo. page, and 3. line for *money* read scarce./ In the last Page, for *conscience*, read *nonsense*" [Sig. (A6v)]). Finally, Sir Gregory begins his account, speaking in loose blank verse:

> It was in Iune the eight and thirtieth day,
> That I imbarked was on highgate Hill.
> After discourteous friendly taking leaue:
> Of my young father *Madge* and Mother *Iobn*,
> The Wind did ebbe, the tide flou'd North South-east,
> We hoist our Sailes of Colloquintida,
> And after 13. dayes and 17. nights,
> (With certaine Hiroglyphicke houres to boote)
> We with tempestuous calmes, and friendly stormes,
> Split our maine top-mast, close below the keele.
>
> [Sig. (A7)]

Rhetorically, Taylor's heavy emphasis on two of the tropes, oxymoron and chiasmus, employed so successfully in *A Midsummer Night's Dream* is evident here. Where Thisbe had bewailed at Pyramus' death the loss of "These Lily lips, / This cherry nose," Sir Gregory crosses his adjectives to produce Father Madge and Mother John as well as tempestuous calms and friendly storms. And in both the proem and body, oxymorons, such as the discourteous friendly taking leave, abound. On his travels, Sir Gregory encounters a succession of unlikely creatures. The first is "A dumbe faire spoken, welfac'd aged youth" (Sig. A7) who delivers a nonsense speech about flying through fabulous places. A fearsome vision next arises and gives Sir Gregory advice, concluding with the piece of wisdom "That nothing kils a man so soone as death" (Sig. [A8v]). This news is snatched up and carried about by Oberon, King of the Fairies, mounted on a wasp, while the weathercock at St. Pancradge's Church makes a speech. Next a German conjuror reads out of a "learned Booke of Palmistry" (Sig. [A8]); as Sir Gregory ponders his meaning "when straite a water Tankerd answer'd me" (Sig. [B1v]). Attention then shifts to Amsterdam where the reader hears "A most learned-Lye, and Illiterate Oration, in lame galloping Rime, fustianly pronounced by Nimshag, a Gimnosophicall Phoolosopher" (Sig. [B2v]). This speech turns out to be an account of the descent of Aesop, "that old fabulistick Phrigian" (Sig. B2), to the underworld where he reports to Pluto on the success of his people on earth. Although a few hold out against his regency, Pluto's followers thrive in Houndsditch, Bridewell, and the stews; Pluto's reply that he doesn't care since they are all fools anyway bypasses the opportunity for any serious social commentary and maintains the tone of light-hearted fooling. Sir Gregory leaves the reader with the assurance that there must be sense in his news somewhere, although the comic effect of his heavy double rhymes belies him:

> Thus do I make a hotch potch messe of *Nonsence*,
> In darke Eniguaes, and strange sence vpon sence:
> It is not foolish all, nor is it wise all,

Nor is it true in all, nor is it lies all.
I haue not shew'd my wits accute or fluent,
Nor told which way of late the wandring Iew went,
For mine owne part I neuer cared greatly,
(So I farewell) where those that dresse the meate lye.

[Sig. (B6v)]

Unfortunately, nowhere in the chapbook does Taylor speak of the class or type of readership at which he aims his anarchic vision. (Taylor includes a postscript to those scholars skilled in classical, modern, and Hebrew languages, noting that they may see from his English that he understands their languages as well as they do his, but of course this is only more of the fooling.) He writes out of the tradition of popular jokes and jestbooks, chapbook heroes and popular entertainments, that were increasingly considered fit only for children, and he employs such comic devices as double rhymes, logical contradictions, non sequiturs, and rhetorical exaggeration that subsequently became staples in nonsense verse written for children. Whether or not Taylor did set out consciously to appeal to young readers among his general audience, his achievement in sustaining the light mood of pure nonsense throughout is remarkable especially for this early date. The journey to the underworld for comment upon human affairs and mock orations are both staples of classical satire, revived in the sixteenth century by Thomas More, Erasmus, and others. But their works are satiric, with a definite target and strategy of attack; Taylor, however, borrows these devices to create a topsy-turvy universe of speaking water tankards, "pragmaticall potato Pies" (Sig. B), and classical heroes like Sisiphus, who is glimpsed dining on "Muskadell and Egges" (Sig. [B7v]). The aim is fun rather than correction, and it is this unity of tone and atmosphere which more than anything makes *Sir Gregory Nonsence* a notable forerunner of the development of nonsense verse written strictly for a juvenile readership.[25]

Like *Sir Gregory Nonsense*, Taylor's final chapbook publication of interest to students of the history of children's literature stands near the beginning of a distinct genre usually associated with the nineteenth century: the story of the faithful animal companion. Around 1628 Taylor published *A Dogge of Warre, or The Travels of Drunkard*, the prototype or great-grandfather of the Lassie stories, and the only one of Taylor's many chapbooks to have been reprinted separately in the twentieth century.[26] The work is a verse encomium of Drunkard, "a little blacke Dogge" depicted resolutely on guard in the title page woodcut, preceded and followed by prose commentary. In his preface, Taylor discusses the animal whose exploits and fidelity are the theme of his verse; he means to extoll the courage and loyalty of the noble dog who travelled to the wars during campaigns in Flanders, Belgium, and finally France with his master, a British soldier of Taylor's acquaintance. Drunkard's distinguished career in the original K-9 corps is detailed and his military bearing commended:

> Two rows of teeth for / Armes he bore,
> Which in his mouth hee / alwaies wore,
> Which serued to fight and / feed too.
> His grumbling for his / Drum did passe,
> And barking (lowd) his / Ordnance was,
> Which help'd in time of / need too.[27]

In the French conflict, however, Drunkard's master was slain. He stands guard over the body until one of his master's companions removes the dead man's cloak. Still guarding his master's property, Drunkard follows the soldier back to the English ships:

So after all his woe / and wracke
To *Westminster* he was / brought backe,
A poore halfe starued / Creature.
And in remembrance of / his cares,
Vpon his backe hee / closely weares,
A mourning Coate by / nature.

[p. 367]

The forlorn animal now haunts the Westminster area where his master had been quartered, sustained by handouts from soldiers and civilians, like the poet, who recall his loyal service.

I lou'd thy master, so / did all

.   .   .   .

For wose (sic) sake, I'le / his dog prefer,
And at the Dogge at / Westminster
Shall *Drunkard* be a / Bencher;
Where I will set a / worke his chaps,
Not with bare bones, or / broken scraps,
But victualls from my / Trencher.

[p. 368]

Taylor concludes the chapbook with a survey of noble beasts from Alexander the Great's horse and the Emperor Augustus's parrot down to a bitch recently discovered by the watermen, Taylor's companions, at Blackfriars, a creature who proves the very pattern of maternal affection in her solicitude for her pups.

Once again, there is no direct evidence of the audience Taylor sought with this publication. According to his own protestations, he writes only to memorialize the animal and the principle of fidelity he symbolizes: "Vpon whose fidelity (for the loue I owed his diseased master) I haue writ these following lines, to expresse my Addiction to the Prouerb,

Loue me and Loue my Hound" (p.363). Taylor's invocation of proverbs here and elsewhere (*e.g.*: "Thus the old Prouerbe is fulfilled. *A Dogge shall haue his day*: And this Dogge hath not out liued his Reputation, but [to the perpetuall renowne of himselfe, and good example of his owne begotten Puppies] hee hath his bright day of Fame perspicuously shining" [p. 369]) bases his story firmly upon oral culture, especially that of the nursery, where children were alternately enticed and warned by such nuggets of folk wisdom.

Taylor's verse (he writes in doggerel "As for a dogge I thought it fit" [p. 364]) also suggests an appeal to beginning readers and those whose tastes had been formed on the songs of the nursery. The broken lines, as indicated by the solidus (/) in the quoted passages, the heavy beats, and comic double rhymes all echo this tradition. Indeed, the combination of Taylor's attitude of affection mixed with humor, his simple verse, attractively illustrated title page, and inexpensive price (no more than one or two pence)[28] would have made his pamphlet most attractive to youthful readers. Taylor's purpose, to defend dogs from "the many petty ridiculous aspersions" cast upon them, would appeal to any schoolboy pet owner, and from such chapbooks as those detailing the exploits of heroes like Sir Bevis of Southampton and his loyal steed Arundel, children were accustomed to reading tales of heroic animal companions. But prior to Taylor's *Dogge of Warre*, the free-standing pet story in attractive and inexpensive format is not to be found.

Perhaps it is not surprising that John Taylor should have initiated three genres which were to become the particular property of children. Taylor was at no time a member of the literary establishment, many of whose members scorned his efforts and mocked him. Instead, to support himself, Taylor had to find, often to create, new audiences among the readers of popular literature and among readers not being serviced by writers from the elite or "literary" culture. His publication record, consequently, maps a series of experiments in all sorts of forms as he sought to discover what would sell and to whom. Writing for a popular audience willing to pay a few pennies to be entertained, Taylor experimented not only with new genres but also with innovative marketing techniques and publication methods. Whether or not he specifically targeted the youthful audience as a potential market we cannot know absolutely, although the internal evidence from his chapbooks suggests, at the least, a concerted effort to appeal to the young members of the general audience. While his *Verbum Sempiternum* helped shape the history of thumb Bibles for children, there is no similar evidence that his contributions to nonsense verse and animal stories had an impact upon the subsequent development of these genres in children's literature. Nevertheless, it was Taylor who first popularized these forms and made them available in attractive and inexpensive format to readers of all ages at the historical period when the concept of entertaining books written for children was taking shape. For this reason, Taylor and his contribution to the development of distinct genres deserve a place in the history of English children's literature.

NINE

Nature Moralized:
John Bunyan's
Country Rhimes for Children

John Bunyan's *A Book for Boys and Girls: Or, Country Rhimes For Children* (1686) is today an almost forgotten work. Even in histories of children's literature it rates little more than footnote treatment; usually, critics are content with two terse observations about the work: children have always much preferred the great *Pilgrim's Progress* to the book Bunyan wrote especially for them and, besides, Bunyan's poetic abilities were slight. While neither observation is completely erroneous, they are very misleading in their suggestion that Bunyan's book is simply juvenile drivel safely dismissed out of hand. In fact, the whole truth is quite different. By exploring the cultural and religious contexts in which Bunyan composed the book, one of the earliest English children's books to aim at entertaining as well as instructing them, and by examining the text of the 1686 edition,[1] I will suggest that *Country Rhimes* has been seriously undervalued as literature for children. My reassessment is based upon two points in particular: historically the book Bunyan wrote has been misread and misrepresented and, second, if Bunyan's verse is not of a very high order, the conception, design, and execution of his children's book is singularly successful in achieving the purposes for which Bunyan wrote it.

As to the first charge, that children have not cared for the *Country Rhimes*, an examination of the very curious textual history of the book illustrates that children have seldom had a chance to read Bunyan's book. The book appeared well after *Pilgrim's Progress* had made Bunyan and his writing famous, and we may assume the press run of *Country Rhimes* was at least of normal size for this popular author. Yet today only a couple of copies of the 1686 *Country Rhimes* survive, the rest presumably having been read to pieces. But if the first edition, Bunyan's book, is very rare, its bastard offspring are not, and it is these that have brought Bunyan's book its poor reputation among both children and critics.[2]

Versions of Bunyan's book were quite popular in the eighteenth century, which witnessed over a dozen editions, often profusely illustrated; but all the eighteenth-century editions mutilate the book, dropping Bunyan's poetical preface, chopping up the poems (deleting especially verses not directly moral in intent), and even changing the title, to *Divine Emblems, or Temporal Things Spiritualized*. The second edition, of 1701, for example, deletes one-third of the poems and rearranges the remaining forty-nine verses. Although there are no surviving copies of the third through eighth editions, an advertisement for the third edition describes it as now "ornamented with cuts," and the ninth edition of 1724, the next of which a copy survives, indeed supplies emblematic woodcuts before many of the poems. The addition of woodcuts must have been the work of a shrewd printer, for by the eighteenth century the emblem tradition had run its course in England, passing from the literati of Spenser's age to the popular Puritan writers of Bunyan's and winding up finally in the nursery as a toy to amuse the young. These various changes in Bunyan's book were evidently made by the trade to give the book more appeal not to children but to their parents, who seem to have preferred that their offspring receive moral instruction unencumbered by charming fancies or poetic flights. At any rate, the mutilated eighteenth-century version is the book children shunned and, until a unique copy of the original 1686 printing was discovered during the nineteenth century, this is the book critics thought Bunyan himself had written.

Bunyan wrote his children's book for the same reason he wrote his other books: to spread the truth of the gospel and save souls. Typically, he announces both his intent and method at the outset of the volume, in his verses entitled "To the Reader":

> Wherefore good Reader, that I save them may,
> I now with them, the very Dottril play.
> And since at Gravity they make a Tush,
> My very Beard I cast behind the Bush,
> And like a Fool stand fing'ring of their Toys;
> And all to shew them, they are Girls and Boys.

He will play with childish subjects with the goal, he continues, "of catching Girls and Boys" and teaching them God's truth. In his concern to instruct the child in righteousness, Bunyan testifies to the strong Puritan interest in the natures of young children. Following the dictates of John Calvin, the English Puritans were convinced of the natural depravity and inherently sinful natures of children; at the same time, Puritan parents loved their offspring no less than parents of other ages and creeds. This ambivalence toward the sinful children they loved led seventeenth-century Puritans to a concentration on children manifested in a fervent desire to convince them of their sinfulness and the need for conversion and regeneration through Christ. Thus, a writer such as John Owen in *A Discourse Concerning the Holy Spirit* (1674) is able to trace the effects of original sin through five clearly marked stages from infancy through youth—unless conversion stops the cancer. And such Puritan authors as Thomas White in *A Little Book for Little Children* (1674) and James Janeway in his infamous *A Token for Children* (1672) exhorted youth through stories alternately morbid and terrifying to impose spiritual discipline upon their lives and to emulate adult conversion patterns popularized by such spiritual autobiographies as Bunyan's classic *Grace Abounding to the Chief of Sinners*. Although *Country Rhimes* does contain a few grim verses, such as "Upon Death" or "Upon the Disobedient Child," for the most part Bunyan's volume partakes of the more humane tradition of Puritan children's books represented by such works as William Jole's *The Father's Blessing* (1674). Bunyan will play the Pauline role of God's fool, writing of childish pastimes and country creatures in order to show how all creation, all activity, is intent with spiritual significance and moral reference if viewed from the Christian perspective. Thus, Bunyan explains, "What tho my Text seems mean, my Morals be / Grave, as if fetcht from a Sublimer Tree."

The book Bunyan wrote for children, and for adults addicted to childish trifles ("artifical Babes," Bunyan calls them), is composed of seventy-four poems written in either couplets or simple cross-rime. For the most part, the verse is competent, though there are certainly tedious patches, such as the opening "Of Moses and his Wife": "This *Moses* was a fair and comely man; / His wife a swarthy Ethiopian." For enduring such turgidity, the persevering reader is often rewarded, however, with lively poetry, plain, vigorous, and laced with broad wit, as in the following verses from "Of the Fatted Swine":

But Hogg, why look'st so big? Why dost so flounce,
So snort, and fling away, dost now renounce
Subjection to thy Lord, 'cause he has fed thee?
Thou art yet but a Hogg, of such he bred thee.
Lay by thy snorting, do not look so big,
What was thy Predecessor but a Pig.

Based on sharp observation, the portrait here fully realizes, in delightful fashion, the creature's attitude, a fit emblem of ungrateful man. And Bunyan's language is direct, concrete, and clean without being watered down or simplified in a negative fashion for consumption by readers of tender years. As his most recent editor affirms, one of the real strengths of *Country Rhimes* is Bunyan's "ability to speak in a voice which children would understand and find attractive . . . a quality which above all distinguishes Bunyan from . . . the tradition of the Baptist poets and writers, among whom were many who produced books of poems and prose for the guidance and edification of children in the seventeenth century."[3] At his best, Bunyan's denotative clarity and simple rhythms "often give the poems," according to Rosemary Freeman, "the spontaneity of a nursery rhyme. The verse has at least the virtues of vigour and economy."[4]

The subject matter of Bunyan's poems is drawn primarily from the sights and sounds of a country child's world (*e.g.*, "On the Kackling of a Hen," "On the Post-boy," "Upon a Penny Loaf," "Upon the Frog," etc.). In this group of poems, the bulk of the collection, Bunyan features a distinctive two-part organization derived from the popular emblem tradition. The object is first described in detail in part one, followed by a second section, set apart and labeled "Comparison," where the meaning of the object in part one is drawn out, moralized, and applied to the life of man. A brief representative example of this type of verse is "Upon the Horse in the Mill":

Horses that work i'th' Mill must hood-wink't be;
For they'l be sick or giddy, if they see.
But keep them blind enough, and they will go
That way which would a seeing Horse undo.

Comparison

Thus 'tis with those that do go *Satan's* Round,
No seeing man can live upon his ground.
Then let us count those unto sin inclin'd,
Either besides their wits, bewitch'd or blind.

The strategy is clearly that of the emblem poets, and both the technique itself and Bunyan's relation to the emblem tradition have been studied in illuminating fashion by Rosemary Freeman, Roger Sharrock, and Lynn Sadler among others.[5] I have little to add to their discussion save to issue a reminder that Bunyan used no illustrations, no pictorial emblems, in the children's book he published. Perhaps neither he nor his printer was able to procure the services of an artist to prepare appropriate woodcuts to adorn the text. Despite his debt to the emblem tradition, however, it also seems possible that Bunyan may have deliberately excluded pictures for the reason that although they constitute an additional appeal and pleasure to the child, pictures both distract attention from the text, i.e., the verbal message, and supply the role the reader's imagination must otherwise fill. This is a point to which I will return momentarily.

In addition to the emblematic treatment of objects from the country child's world, Bunyan includes verse paraphrases of the Lord's Prayer and Creed and didactic religious verses such as "Upon the Sacraments" and "Of the Love of Christ." There are also a handful of poems on such abstractions as Death and Beauty and a few on such Biblical topics as Moses and his wife and the spouse of Christ. All of these diverse subjects, abstract and concrete, Biblical and bucolic, are fodder for Bunyan in his attempt to win young souls through verse by showing them the meaning and application of their quotidian surroundings.

In bringing these poems together into *Country Rhimes*, I suggest that Bunyan seeks to initiate children into a particular way of seeing the world, both in individual poems and in the volume as a whole. In "Upon the Horse in the Mill," quoted earlier, Bunyan uses the blinkered horse as an emblem of people caught in Satan's toils, blinded spirits who plod in circles without realizing their lack of progress or true direction. The verses in *Country Rhimes* are designed to save children from the life portrayed in this negative emblem, to teach them to see allegorically, in a double vision. Thus, poems such as "Whipping a Top," "The Swallow," and the others interpret the customary materials of a child's experience as moral hieroglyphs, reflecting the Puritan belief in a world in which every act, every creature, is charged with moral significance. This bifurcated vision stretches in literature back through the emblems and allegories of the Renaissance through the figurative interpretations of the medieval sermon, and into the roots of Christianity itself. While the Puritans are distinctive primarily in the great stress they lay on this typological or allegorical mode of seeing, it is an essential view of the world which they attempted to teach their children through sermons, devotions, tracts, and books of various kinds. Thus, it is not surprising that Bunyan writes poetry whose sharp descriptions and attached "comparisons" show the godly child how to appreciate his world even as he develops and benefits from this sacramental vision. By using the images of childhood and the stuff of a child's experience, couched in a basic vocabulary and attractive rhymed verse, Bunyan meets the child on his level with an entertaining introduction to the religion and cultural perspective of the adult Protestant world.

Indeed, I suggest that in his attempt to "catch" or save young souls by showing them how to see rightly, Bunyan ordered his small volume of verse in a manner calculated to draw the child into the work and provide him successively with the tools required for godly vision. I believe there are definite patterns to the topics chosen for versification and to their arrangement in the volume, patterns lost after the first edition as a result of the omission of some poems and rearrangement of others by eighteenth-century editors interested primarily in the pictures and mainstream popular piety desired by the book-buying public. To my knowledge, the presence of system and order in *Country Rhimes* has never been suggested;[6] thus, I will examine briefly one section of the volume which I believe exhibits a distinctive pattern.

In explaining his strategy in the prefatory poem, "To the Reader," Bunyan says, "by their *Play-things*, I would them entice, / To mount their Thoughts from what are childish Toys, / To Heav'n, for that's prepar'd for Girls and Boys." Through revealing the divine in the quotidian, he will teach their thoughts to mount. But before Bunyan's method can operate to correct a child's vision and show him how to see double, both the object and its moral significance, two requirements must be met. First, the child must be entertained, or at least instructed pleasantly, to ensure his voluntary attention to the poet-preacher's message. Second, double vision is not just an allegorical game; it is based on theological principles and religious belief. A child needs to be taught the basics of faith as an ethical guide and spiritual anchor to show him how and why he must look beyond the surface of things. An examination of the structure of Bunyan's volume of verse reveals it to be carefully ordered so as to fulfill these essential preliminaries and proceed, utilizing a pleasing variety of forms, to instruct the reader in ways of seeing rightly.

Knowing children's natural curiosity about the mysterious process of reading, Bunyan begins by providing basic aids for them. Although *Country Rhimes* is not, in any ordinary or pedagogical sense, a textbook, Bunyan opens his volume with a page entitled "An help to Chil-dren to learn to read English." He includes charts of the alphabet printed in different characters and scripts, tables of vowels, spelling aids, and advice on syllabification. The following page, entitled "To learn Chil-dren to spell a-right their names," lists fifty-eight of the most common names of boys and girls broken into syllables. Finally, a third page of introductory material is headed "To learn Children to know Figures, and Numeral Letters," featuring charts of figures and Arabic and Roman numerals. In this three-page prefatory section, Bunyan meets the child where he is, offering simplified basic instruction in the alphabet and syllables, a lesson immediately rewarded by the table of children's names. A father himself, Bunyan knew the first word a child would wish to spell and write would be his own name. The utility of the tables of figures to the child is obvious, even if their presence in a volume of verse may seem odd, as it apparently did to Bunyan's eighteenth-century editors who cut the entire prefatory apparatus. But Bunyan is giving the child essential instructional material, mixing the instruction of the tables with the child's pleasure in learning to write his own name and, in the process, favorably disposing the child to what comes after. That Bunyan's purpose in this prefatory section is not simply pedagogical, as a supplement to the hornbooks, but religious, is evident in his concluding comment that "I shall forbear to add more, being perswaded this is enough for little children to prepare themselves for Psalter, or Bible." From Bunyan's perspective, reading is primarily a tool to unlock the wisdom of Scripture.

Bunyan's volume of poetry proper begins with a versification of the Ten Commandments, casting them into rhymed couplets for facility of retention by children. Thus he begins his book with the essentials of the Old Law, the Decalogue, which every good Christian should keep in his memory as a guide to living. "Upon the Ten Commandments" is followed by "The Awakened Child's Lamentation," a dramatic monologue in twenty-nine four-line stanzas. The poetics of this poem are most interesting and unusual when considered in the context of Bunyan's ordinary practice. Metrically he employs a trimeter line ending each line of a stanza with the same double rhyme. The form creates a breathless effect, each short line gasped out by the young speaker, with special emphasis placed on the quickly recurring rhyme words, reinforced by the double rhymes. The content is still more interesting, however, for in some respects the poem may be seen as paradigmatic; Bunyan himself is writing for "awakened" children who, like the speaker of the poem, have become aware of their sinfulness and seek guidance into the paths of righteousness. Confession of the sort represented by the awakened child's speech should precede instruction in the Puritan world-view; then follows the set of instructions Bunyan's verses offer in how the world shows God's handiwork and offers lessons compatible with the teaching of ministers, parents, and schoolmasters, if only the child can learn to read it right. But first the child must read *himself* aright. He must recognize, with the awakened child, that

> O Lord! I am ashamed,
> When I do hear thee named;
> 'Cause thee I have defamed,
> And liv'd like Beasts untamed.

Of course some people, who will neither hear nor see, are lost, but for the awakened child there is hope, for

> Lord! thou wast crucified
> For Sinners, bled and dyed,
> I have for Mercy cryed,
> Let me not be denyed.

Thus, even as the child learns of the grand division between those who will and will not see, he is assured that despite his own wanton and sinful nature, there is hope for his soul if he can learn to read aright, for Christ's atonement and God's mercy are sufficient to save him. Thus, the consolation of the poem's conclusion:

> But God has condescended,
> And pardon has extended,
> To such as have offended,
> Before their lives were ended.
>
> O Lord! do not disdain me,
> But kindly entertain me;
> Yea in thy faith maintain me,
> And let thy Love constrain me.

In the opening verses of *Country Rhimes*, the child learns the rules of Christian conduct and the necessity for acknowledging his past failure to live as he should as a condition for the salvation promised God's people. Following these preparatory steps, he is ready for initiation into the Puritan way of seeing, a process illustrated in the third poem in the volume, "Meditation Upon an Egg." Here in a clear, logical fashion which respects the intelligence of his target audience, Bunyan shows how meditating on the Book of Creatures can lead to true vision. Instead of the two-part organization characteristic of his emblem poems, in "Meditation Upon an Egg" Bunyan illustrates no less than fourteen points of similitude between an egg and the moral life of man, setting them out for the most part in economical distiches, as in the opening lines:

> The Egg's no Chick by falling from the Hen;
>   Nor man a Christian, till he's born agen.
> The Egg's at first contained in the Shell;
>   Men afore Grace, in sins, and darkness dwell.

The poem is something of a tour de force in working out the parallels so exhaustively, but if it does nothing else, the poem illustrates how rich even so mundane and unpromising a subject as an egg may be when viewed from an awakened Protestant perspective. And although the eighteenth-century editors preface the verse with a woodcut of a hen and egg, the poem is wholly self-contained, requiring no addition. Indeed, for the purpose of Puritan meditation,[7] the poem works better without the illustration by forcing the child to bring his imagination to bear along with his heart and mind on the object set for him by the poet. Bunyan's description is sufficiently specific and palpable to illumine the focused faculties of the reader on its own terms. Meanwhile, thematically, "Meditation Upon an Egg" echoes the theme of redemption and the prospect of salvation for the penitent announced in "The Awakened Child's Lamentation." Puritan doctrine can seem very cold and forbidding; Bunyan seeks to soften without distortion in his poems for the young. The lure of Christ's love is preferred to threats of Hell.

While a youthful reader would learn of the rich possibilities of the allegorical mode of seeing from "Meditation Upon an Egg," by its very success in finding similitudes the poem might discourage the apprentice reader. How is a child to see so much in his surroundings? He will require aid, even more than the poet can provide through precept and example. Thus, the fourth poem in *Country Rhimes* is a versification of the Lord's Prayer, a reminder to the child of the ultimate source of all aid. After the reminder that God will aid the partial or weak sight of the devout, Bunyan places two brief poems, "Meditation upon Peep of day" and "Upon the Flint in the Water." These poems are much simpler than "Meditation Upon an Egg," showing how inanimate aspects of Creation, daybreak and a stone in water, can yield moral significance when viewed rightly. And in their simplicity and brevity, the poems both offer welcome variety from contiguous long verses such as "The Awakened Child's Lamentation" or "Meditations upon the Candle" and so inspire confidence in the youthful reader that the new way of seeing is not too complex and difficult to be mastered, as "Meditation Upon an Egg" might have suggested.

In the next three poems, "Upon the Fish in the Water," "Upon the Swallow," and "Upon the Bee," Bunyan moves up the Chain of Being from inanimate to animate creation. Again, the poems are brief, emblematic treatments of the Book of Creatures. Prior to the next step up in the progression Bunyan is tracing, the examination of man in his moral aspects, Bunyan places two poems between "Upon the Bee" and the poems which deal directly with man, such as "Upon over-much Niceness," "The Sinner and the Spider," and others. First is "Upon the Creed," a versification of the Apostles' Creed to remind the young reader of the central tenets of his faith, and "Upon a low'ring Morning," an emblematic poem which plays on the paradox of appearance and reality. Here the threatening morning, dark and streaked with "slabby Rain," is, when properly viewed in the Comparison, seen to be a positive emblem of the Atonement:

> Thus 'tis when Gospel-light doth usher in
> To us, both sense of Grace, and sense of Sin;
> Yea when it makes sin red with Christ's blood,
> Then can we weep, till weeping does us good.

With this final reminder that the appearance of the physical world is deceptive unless read rightly by the penitent

Christian, Bunyan is ready for the verses that compose the center of his collection, poems on man and the creatures, including several long, important poems such as "Meditations upon the Candle," "The Sinner and the Spider," and "Of the Child with the Bird at the Bush." Eventually, Bunyan concludes his collection with "Of Beauty," a brief poem reminding the child reader that " 'Tis but skin-deep, and therefore must decay"; but by this time, the child should have learned how to read in Puritan fashion, reflexively looking beyond the decaying or deceptive surface to the Christian truth suggested by the topic.

In summary, I suggest that *Country Rhimes* is a more complex, successful, and important book than has been recognized. A reexamination of the first edition, the book Bunyan wrote, offers evidence not only of a central theme controlling the selection of subjects for versification but also of careful patterning, psychological and theological, of a number of poems in the volume. If my reading of the volume is correct, then in these poems Bunyan's real achievement is to introduce to children a way of seeing their lives and the world, a way of interpreting their experience according to a practical theology shared by adults, without condescension or apology, in entertaining yet explicit fashion. The country preacher played the fool both wisely and well.

Notes

1. From Caxton to Comenius

1. Among the best recent studies of Caxton are N.F. Blake, *Caxton: England's First Publisher* (New York: Barnes & Noble, 1976) and George D. Painter, *William Caxton: A Quincentenary Biography of England's First Printer* (London: Chatto & Windus, 1976); also useful are Frieda E. Penninger, *William Caxton* (New York: Twayne, 1979) and A.T.P. Byles, "William Caxton as a Man of Letters," *The Library*, series 4, 15 (1934), 1-25.

2. See Arthur F. Leach, *The Schools of Medieval England* (London: Methuen, 1915) and Kenneth Charlton, *Education in Renaissance England* (London: Routledge & Kegan Paul, 1965) for standard studies of the school curriculum of the period.

3. Elyot, for example, urges the master: "After a fewe and quicke rules of grammer, immediately, or interlasynge it therwith, wolde be redde to the childe Esopes fables in greke: in which argument children moche do delite. And surely it is a moche pleasant lesson and also profitable, as well for that it is elegant and brefe, (and nat withstanding it hath moche varietie in wordes, and therwith moche helpeth to the understandinge of greke) as also in those fables is included moche morall and politike wisedome." Thomas Elyot, *The Book Named the Governor*, 1531 (Menston: Scolar Press, 1970), [Fol. 31v].

4. See David G. Hale, "Aesop in Renaissance England," *The Library*, 27 (1972), 116-25.

5. *Caxton's Book of Curtesye*. Ed. Frederick J. Furnivall (London: Early English Text Society, 1868), p. 2.

6. Ibid., p. 53.

7. E. Duff Gordon, "England," in A.W. Pollard, *Early Illustrated Books* (London: Kegan Paul, 1917), p. 219. For further discussion of Caxton's use of illustrations, see Arthur M. Hind, *An Introduction to a History of Woodcut* (1935; rpt., New York: Dover, 1963), 2: 706-14.

8. It is interesting to note that the foremost among Humanist educational reformers, Erasmus, called specifically for the printing of illustrated texts of Aesop to be used for the education of youth. In *De Pueris Instituendis* (1529), for example, he argues that "for fables and apologues, the child will more willingly learn them and remember them better if the subjects are presented to him before his very eyes, cleverly illustrated, and if all that the story relates is shown to him in the picture." Quoted in Jean-Claude Margolin, "The Method of 'Words and Things' in Erasmus's *De Pueris Instituendis* (1529) and Comenius's *Orbis Sensualium Pictus* (1658)," in *Essays on the Works of Erasmus*, ed. Richard L. DeMolen (New Haven: Yale University Press, 1978), p. 226. For a consideration of manuscript illustrations of Aesop before the invention of printing, see Georg Thiele, *Der illustrierte lateinische Aesop in der Handschrift des Ademar. Codex Vossianus. Lat. Oct. 15. Fol. 195-205* (Leiden: A.W. Sitjhoff, 1905).

9. For a further discussion of the basic elements of the fables' appeal specifically to children, see Robert G. Miner, Jr., "Aesop as Litmus: The Acid Test of Children's Literature," *Children's Literature*, 1 (1972): 9-15.

10. Edward Hodnett, *Aesop in England: The Transmission of Motifs in Seventeenth-Century Illustrations of Aesop's Fables* (Charlottesville: Univ. Press of Virginia, 1979), p. 17.

11. *The Acts and Monuments of John Foxe*, ed. S.R. Cattley and George Townsend, rev. ed. (1843-49; rpt. New York: AMS Press, 1965), 1:viii. All future citations of *The Book of Martyrs* will be to this edition with volume and page numbers included in the text.

12. Thomas White, *A Little Book for Little Children*. 12th edition (London: Thomas Parkhurst, 1702), pp. 17-18. For a representative sampling of Renaissance clergymen and teachers who enthusiastically recommended the *Book of Martyrs* to young readers, see the comments by Thomas Fuller, James Janeway, Richard Baxter,

and others cited in William Sloane, *Children's Books in England and America in the Seventeenth Century* (New York: Columbia Univ. Press, 1955).

13. J.F. Mozley, *John Foxe and His Book* (1940; rpt., New York: Octagon Books, 1970), commentary on print facing p. 117.

14. See Frances Yates, *Astraea: The Imperial Theme in the Sixteenth Century* (London: Routledge and Kegan Paul, 1975), especially p. 44.

15. *The Book of Martyrs*, ed. George Williamson (Boston: Little, Brown, 1966), p. xx. For a thoughtful discussion of the uses of idealized or "iconic" illustrations and apparently "realistic" ones in children's books of the fifteenth and sixteenth centuries, I am indebted to Patricia Dooley for a prepublication copy of her essay, "Icons for Infants: Some Questions Raised by Late Medieval and Renaissance Illustrated Children's Books."

16. According to a story related in Sir John Harington's *A Brief View of the State of the Church of England*, someone thinking to irritate Bonner showed him the woodcut depicting him scourging a martyr in his garden. Bonner is supposed to have replied with a laugh: "A vengeance on the fool! How could he get my picture drawn so right?" (Quoted in Mozley, *John Foxe and His Book*, p. 131).

17. There is an interesting discussion of this latter engraving in Elizabeth H. Hageman, "John Foxe's Henry VIII as *Justitia*," *The Sixteenth Century Journal*,/, 1 (Spring, 1979):35-44.

18. For an extended treatment of *The Book of Martyrs* as a children's book, see chapter 5.

19. The best recent work on Comenius is by John E. Sadler whose *J.A. Comenius and the Concept of Universal Education* (New York: Barnes & Noble, 1966) and his introductory commentary in *Comenius* (London: Macmillan, 1969) are both very useful. Older studies chiefly valuable for their discussion of the biographical context of Comenius's writings are Simon S. Laurie, *John Amos Comenius, Bishop of the Moravians: His Life and Educational Works* (London: Kegan Paul, Trench & Co., 1881) and Will S. Monroe, *Comenius and the Beginnings of Educational Reform* (1900; rpt., New York: Arno Press, 1971). The most comprehensive survey of Comenius's relationship

to the growth of children's literature is E.W. Davidson, "*Orbis Pictus:* Comenius' Contributions to Children's Literature," Ph.D. dissertation, Catholic University of America, 1958.

20. Jan Amos Comenius, *Orbis Sensualium Pictus,* 1659. Translated by Charles Hoole (Menston: Scolar Press, 1970), Sig. A4. All future citations of the *Orbis Pictus* will be to this edition with page numbers included in the text.

21. "The spectacle of the world and of all the creatures inhabiting it requires the total participation of the child spectator, and to his active and scrutinizing gaze corresponds a dynamic experience of vocabulary, through the fixation in the memory of short sentences which are themselves elements of action." Jean-Claude Margolin, "The Method of 'Words and Things' in Erasmus's *De Pueris Instituendis* (1529) and Comenius's *Orbis Sensualium Pictus* (1658)," p. 234.

2. Childermass Sermons in Late Medieval England

1. The standard sources for information on the background, antiquity, and customs of the celebration of Holy Innocents' Day in England are the accounts in E. K. Chambers, *The Medieval Stage* (1903), Vol. 1, A. F. Leach, "The Schoolboys' Feast," *Fortnightly,* January, 1896, and Karl Young, *The Drama of the Medieval Church* (1935). A study which explores some continental Boy Bishop customs, which persisted in parts of France into the eighteenth century, is Natalie Z. Davis, "The Reasons of Misrule: Youth Groups and Charivaris in Sixteenth-Century France," *Past and Present,* 50 (Feb., 1971): 41-75. While I am indebted to all these studies in my discussion of the Childermass customs, I have not been able to locate or consult W.C. Meller's *The Boy Bishop and Other Essays on Forgotten Customs and Beliefs of the Past* (London, 1923).

2. See, for example, the discussion of the Feast of the Ass and the Childermass ceremonies in C.M. Gayley's *Plays of Our Forefathers and Some of the Traditions upon which They Were Founded* (1907; rpt. N.Y.: Biblo and Tannen, 1968).

3. The relevant passages are conveniently included in an appendix to Karl Young's *The Drama of the Medieval Church.*

4. Quoted in A.F. Leach, "The Schoolboy's Feast," p. 139.

5. Quoted in Leach, p. 137.

6. Quoted in Leach, p. 136.

7. Quoted in G.R. Owst, *Preaching in Medieval England* (1926; rpt. Russell & Russell, 1965), p. 220.

8. Chambers notes the existence of a *Sermo pro episcopo puerorum* printed by R. Pynson in the 15th century, now lost, by one J. Alcock (*The Medieval Stage* 1: 356n).

9. "Two Sermons Preached By the Boy Bishop." Introduction and Notes by Edward F. Rimbault. *The Camden Society Miscellany,* 7 (1875). Future citations of these two sermons will be to this edition and page references will be included in the text.

10. This assumption, explicit in Gayley, Chambers, and Leach, is implicit in almost all studies of the matter.

11. A *Sermon of the Chylde Jesus made by the most famous clerke Doctour Erasmus of Roterdā.* (London: W. Redman, 1540), p. Aii. All future citations of the sermon will be to this edition and will be included in the text.

12. J.W. Blench, *Preaching in England in the Late 15th and 16th Centuries* (New York: Barnes and Noble, 1964), p. 166.

3. Childhood and Death

1. Quoted in Nan C. Carpenter, *John Skelton* (New York: Twayne Publishing Co., 1967), p. 66.

2. See, for example, Ian A. Gordon, *John Skelton, Poet Laureate* (Melbourne: Melbourne University Press, 1943) and Robert Kinsman, " 'Phyllyp Sparowe': Titulus," *Studies in Philology,* 47 (1950): 473-84.

3. C.S. Lewis, *English Literature in the Sixteenth Century Excluding Drama* (Oxford: Oxford University Press, 1954), p. 138.

4. H.L.R. Edwards, *Skelton: The Life and Times of an Early Tudor Poet* (1949; rpt. Freeport, N.Y.: Books for Libraries Press, 1971), pp. 102-14. On Jane's background, see also Melvin J. Tucker, "Skelton and Sheriff Hutton," *English Language Notes* 4 (1966-67): 254-59.

5. Although corroborative evidence is lacking, Edwards spec-

ulates that Jane might have witnessed the execution with her mother, Lady Wyndham, who would probably have been required to attend (Skelton: Life and Times), p. 104.

6. Edwards prefers an early date, 1504-05, but such scholars as F.W. Brownlow ("The Boke of Phyllyp Sparowe and the Liturgy," English Literary Renaissance 9, 1 [Winter, 1979]: 5-20) and Nan Carpenter seem to have the better of the argument in suggesting a later date. The only sure dates are the terminal ones: the poem must have been written after 1502 when Jane arrived at Carrow and before 1508 when she married and left the nunnery.

7. "It was very rash for parents to get too emotionally involved with or concerned about creatures whose expectation of life was so very low. Nothing better illustrates this resigned acceptance of the expendability of children than the medieval practice of giving the same name to two living siblings in the expectation that only one would survive." Lawrence W. Stone, The Family, Sex and Marriage in England, 1500-1800 (New York: Harper and Row, 1977), p. 70. Other studies which arrive at the same conclusion include Ivy Pinchbeck and Margaret Hewitt, Children in English Society, Vol. I: From Tudor Times to the 18th Century (London: Routledge and Kegan Paul, 1969) and Philippe Aries, Centuries of Childhood: A Social History of Family Life (New York: A.A. Knopf, 1967).

8. The importance of this ritualistic antiphony has recently been explored in illuminating fashion by F.W. Brownlow in "The Boke of Phyllyp Sparowe and the Liturgy."

9. Lloyd DeMause, "The Evolution of Childhood" in The History of Childhood (New York: The Psychohistory Press, 1974), pp. 51-52.

10. Edwards, Skelton: Life and Times, pp. 102ff.

11. Burton Fishman, "Recent Studies in Skelton," English Literary Renaissance, Vol. I (1971), pp. 89-90.

12. Lewis, English Literature in the Sixteenth Century, p. 138; Stanley Fish, John Skelton's Poetry (New Haven: Yale University Press, 1965), p. 103.

13. Carpenter, John Skelton, p. 60.

14. "Phyllyp Sparowe," ll.1-16 in The Anchor of Sixteenth-Century

Verse, ed. R.S. Sylvester (Garden City, N.Y.: Anchor Books, 1974), p. 23. All citations of the poem will be to this edition with line numbers cited in the text.

15. Erik H. Erikson, *Young Man Luther: A Study in Psychoanalysis and History* (New York: W.W. Norton, 1962), p. 14.

16. This interpretation of the Bird Mass as a direct outgrowth of the psychological and thematic movement of the poem is thus opposed to such readings as that of L.J. Lloyd, who argues that there is no organic relation between the parts of the poem (*John Skelton* [Oxford, 1938]), or Fish's view that the Bird Mass is an escapist digression from Jane's sorrow (*John Skelton's Poetry*).

17. Edwards, *Skelton: Life and Times*, p. 108.

4. The Topos of Childhood in Marian England

1. On the changing concept of education among the gentry, see J.H. Hexter, "The Education of the Aristocracy in the Renaissance," *Reappraisals in History* (Evanston, Ill., 1961), pp. 45-70. For a survey of the broader aspects of the rise of schools in the sixteenth century, see the discussion in Ivy Pinchbeck and Margaret Hewitt, *Children in English Society: Vol. I. From Tudor Times to the Eighteenth Century* (London: 1969).

2. John Calvin, *A Harmonie upon the three Euangelistes, Matthewe, Marke, and Luke, with the Commentarie of M. Iohn Caluine*, trans. E.P. (London: 1610), p. 485.

3. John Calvin, *The Institution of Christian Religion*, trans. Thomas Norton (London, 1611), Bk. II, ch. I, pp. 107-8.

4. Leah S. Marcus, *Childhood and Cultural Despair: A Theme and Variations in Seventeenth-Century Literature* (Pittsburgh, 1978), p. 71. Marcus's study features two introductory chapters on childhood in the Middle Ages and Renaissance which contain much useful information on the sixteenth century.

5. See esp., Phillipe Aries, *Centuries of Childhood: A Social History of Family Life* (New York, 1962).

6. Quoted from the manuscript in the Vatican Library by

Dermot Fenlon in *Heresy and Obedience in Tridentine Italy: Cardinal Pole and the Counter Reformation* (Cambridge, 1972), p. 254.

7. Quoted from Pole's vernacular homilies in Blench, *Preaching in England*, p. 50.

8. Ibid., p. 51.

9. Jasper Ridley, *The Life and Times of Mary Tudor* (London, 1973), p. 82.

10. John Foxe, *Acts and Monuments of These Latter and Perilous Days* . . . (London, 1563), p. 870.

11. Given the difficulty of her childhood and adolescence, it is also possible to interpret Mary's interest in childhood and adolescence, especially an idealized childhood of innocence and harmony, in psychological terms. William Haller moves in this direction when he observes: "When after [the death of Edward VI] Mary came to the throne, hoping to restore religion, she had every personal reason for wishing to go back to the order of things she had known in childhood before her father repudiated his marriage to her mother and embarked on the sequence of changes which brought both women nothing but humiliation and grief. Mary remained to the end a devout Catholic of simple, intense, unquestioning faith, emotionally dependent on her mother's kindred and Spanish countrymen." *The Elect Nation: The Meaning and Relevance of Foxe's "Book of Martyrs"* (New York, 1963), pp. 21-22.

12. Quoted from a manuscript in the Vatican Library by Fenlon in *Heresy and Obedience*, p. 286.

13. Leonard Pollard, *Fyve Homiles of late, made by a ryght good a. vertuous clerke, called Master L. Pollarde* (London, 1556), sigs. E2r-E3v. Pollard expands at length on the topos, distinguishing the three chief points, "chyldyshe simplicitie," utter dependence on God, and "louynge obedience," of childhood which adult Christians should emulate. These he sets forth in schematic fashion: "Remember the dredful day of judgement, when ye rebellious children must apere before hym. Here then maye you see that to beleue in god is fyrst: that as simple children do knowne no person but hym and all thynges by hym. The seconde is, that as the chylde hangeth altogether upn the prouysion of his parentes, and sheweth his

nedes to theym: the like must we do to hym in whom we do beleue. The thyrde, as the chylde is ruled by his parenets chiefely of loue, and where that wanteth, for feare of punyshement: in lyke maner must they do that beleue in God [sig. E2v].

14. *The Diary of Henry Machyn, Citizen and Merchant-Taylor of London, From A.D.* 1550 *to A.D.* 1563, ed. John G. Nichols, Camden Society, Series I, 42 (London, 1848), pp. 80-81.

15. David Bevington, *Tudor Drama and Politics: A Critical Approach to Topical Meaning* (Cambridge, Mass., 1968), p. 118.

16. *Respublica: An Interlude for Christmas* 1553, *Attributed to Nicholas Udall.* Ed. W.W. Greg (London, 1952), pp. ix-x.

17. Ibid., p. 2.

18. Chambers, *Medieval Stage* 1:367.

19. See Chambers, Leach, and Young as cited in Chapter 1. See also Richard L. De Molen, *"Pueri Christi Imitatio:* The Festival of the Boy-Bishop in Tudor England," *Moreana* 45 (Feb. 1975), 17-28.

20. Foxe, p. 757.

21. The relevant passages are conveniently included in an appendix to Karl Young's *The Drama of the Medieval Church.*

22. In 1555 the visitations of the Boy Bishop from St. Paul's included a royal audience where the boy sang a song written for the occasion. Apparently this is another literary elaboration of the ceremony during the Marian period, for there is no mention of any such song in the orders for the St. Nicholas or Childermass feasts. But according to Thomas Warton, Hugh Rhodes, a gentleman of the royal chapel, "printed a poem consisting of thirty-six octave stanzas, entitled 'The SONG of the CHYLDBYSSHOP, as it was songe before the queenes maiestie in her priuie chamber at her manour of saynt James in the ffeeldes on saynt Nicholas day and Innocents day this yeare now present, by the childe bysshope of Poules churche with his company. LONDINI, in aedibus Johannis Cawood, typographi reginae, 1555.' " Although it has not survived, Warton had apparently seen this poem for he describes it as "a fulsome panegyric on the queen's devotion, in which she is compared to Judith, Esther, the queen of Sheba, and the virgin Mary." *The History of English Poetry,* new ed. (London, 1824). 4:146-47.

23. "Two Sermons Preached By the Boy Bishop." Page references in the following discussion are to this edition.

24. Richard Hooker, *Of the Lawes of Ecclesiastical Politie,* 3d ed. (London, 1611), Bk. III, p. 98.

5. John Foxe's *Book of Martyrs* and the Child Reader

1. See, for example, F.J.H. Darton, *Children's Books in England: Five Centuries of Social Life* (Cambridge: University Press, 1932; rpt. 1958), p. 56; and Zena Sutherland and May Hill Arbuthnot, *Children and Books,* 5th ed. (Glenview, Illinois: Scott Foresman and Co., 1977), pp. 40-42.

2. *Foxe's Book of Martyrs, . . . With Notes, Comments, and Illustrations,* by Rev. J. Milner, M.A. (London: Partridge and Oakey, 1850), p. iii.

3. Leslie M. Oliver dispels the common misconception that the *Acts and Monuments* was required in *all* Elizabethan churches, examining the Canon law and the size of the press runs of the sixteenth century English editions in "The Seventh Edition of John Foxe's *Acts and Monuments,*" *PBSA,* 37 (1943): 243-60.

4. William Haller, *The Elect Nation: The Meaning and Relevance of Foxe's Book of Martyrs* (New York: Harper and Row, 1963), pp. 13-14.

5. The tight integration of engraving and text is also quite unusual at this date in English publishing. Note that Foxe has so far designed the pictures and text to support each other and that he calls attention in his text to the appended engravings as, for example, in his description of the terrible martyrdom of John Lambert, where he adds that the martyr died "after the manner and form that is described in the picture adjoined" (5:236).

6. Helen C. White, *Tudor Books of Saints and Martyrs* (Madison: University of Wisconsin Press, 1967), p. 160.

6. Michael Drayton's *Nymphidia*

1. Darton, *Children's Books in England,* p. 1. The usual critical procedure is to ignore altogether the pre-adult portion of the Renaissance reading public. Even such standard studies of the

Renaissance English reading audience as Louis B. Wright's, *Middle-Class Culture in Elizabethan England* (1935) and Edwin H. Miller's *The Professional Writer in Elizabethan England: A Study of Non-dramatic Literature* (1959) avoid any discussion of children and their reading habits.

2. *The British Essayists.* ed. A. Chalmers (Boston: Little, Brown and Co., 1856). II. 363.

3. Katherine M. Briggs, *The Fairies in English Tradition and Literature* (Chicago: Univ. of Chicago Press, 1967). p. 175.

4. Darton, *Children's Books in England*, p. 33.

5. Oliver Elton, *Michael Drayton: A Critical Study* (New York: Russell and Russell, 1966), p. 137.

6. As late as 1909, for example. Drayton was still accorded a full chapter in the *Cambridge History of English Literature.*

7. *The Works of Michael Drayton,* ed. J. William Hebel. (Oxford: Shakespeare Head Press, 1961), 5:202. On the popularity of Drayton in his own day, see Bernard H. Newdigate. *Michael Drayton and His Circle* (Oxford: Shakespeare Head Press, 1961) and Joseph A. Berthelot, *Michael Drayton* (New York: Twayne, 1967). For the fullest survey of Drayton's reputation and the publication history of the poetry see Russell Noyes. *Michael Drayton's Literary Vogue since 1631* (Bloomington: Univ. of Indiana Press, 1935).

8. Richard F. Hardin. *Michael Drayton and the Passing of Elizabethan England* (Lawrence: Univ. Press of Kansas, 1973), p. 133.

9. *The Works of Michael Drayton,* 125. Subsequent citations from *Nymphidia* are to this edition with line numbers cited in the text.

10. Lillian H. Smith, *The Unreluctant Years: A Critical Approach to Children's Literature* (Chicago: American Library Association, 1953). p. 101.

11. See, for example, the discussion of Drayton's indebtedness in *Nymphidia* to Shakespeare in Minor White Latham, *The Elizabethan Fairies* (1930; reprt. New York: Octagon Books, 1972), pp. 203-06.

12. The term is Katherine M. Briggs's in *The Anatomy of Puck: An Examination of Fairy Beliefs among Shakespeare's Contemporaries and Successors* (London: Routledge and Kegan Paul, 1959), p. 58.

13. The objection that the plot of *Nymphidia* in its strong suggestion of adultery in the love triangle likely would not have interested or suited children seems specious. The theme does not seem to have kept Renaissance children from finding their way to Malory's *Morte d'Arthur,* for example, where the subject is treated far more seriously and graphically than in Drayton's poem, where it functions as merely the hinge for the mock-heroic burlesque. And Drayton's handling of the theme is light and deftly humorous without the salacious innuendo found, for example, in some of Herrick's fairy verse.

14. While diminished in most modern studies, attempts to extrapolate a "moral" from *Nymphidia* are not altogether past. Richard Hardin, for example, commenting on the poem's denouement where the timely application of Lethe water heals all wounds with the balm of forgetfulness, spies a useful lesson: "For men, whose bloodiest quarrels have origins that are usually just as insubstantial as the fairies', the implications are clear: almost all the kinds of problems met with in society . . . would vanish were it not for our memory of them. . . . With the detached, ironic view of man's pride and prejudice that is typical of his last years, Drayton has taken a momentary excursion into a world where the ancient curse of memory can be dispelled" (*Michael Drayton and the Passing of Elizabethan England.* p. 74).

15. *Ibid.,* p. v.

7. A Child's Garden of Sprites

1. The standard sources for background information on fairy lore and literature during the English Renaissance are Floris Delattre, *English Fairy Poetry: From the Origins to the Seventeenth Century* (London: Henry Frowde, 1912), Minor W. Latham, *The Elizabethan Fairies* (New York: Octagon Books, 1972; orig. 1930), and the various studies of Katherine M. Briggs, especially her *Anatomy of Puck* and *Fairies in English Tradition and Literature.*

2. Latham, *Elizabethan Fairies,* p. 18n.

3. See James I, *Daemonologie,* 1597. The English Experience

Series, No. 94 (New York: Da Capo Press, 1969), pp. 73-77. In the belief that fairies were hellish spirits, James draws close to the doctrine of his Puritan antagonists, who made little distinction between witches and fairies as demonic agents. As Floris Delattre notes, the Puritans "regarded Fairyland as a province of Satan's immense kingdom, and as one of the most detestable inventions of the Papists" (*English Fairy Poetry,* p. 184). Indeed, the Puritans were so hostile to fairies and fairy lore that their zealousness was sometimes blamed, as in Bishop Richard Corbet's "The Fairies Farewell" (1647), for driving the spirits from England.

4. Egoff, *Republic of Childhood,* p. 8.

5. Smith, *Unreluctant Years,* p. 101.

6. Briggs, *The Fairies in English Tradition and Literature,* p. 115.

7. *The Arte of English Poesie, 1589.* The English Experience Series, No. 342 (New York: Da Capo Press, 1971), pp. 143-44.

8. Latham, *The Elizabethan Fairies,* p. 223.

9. William Empson, *Some Versions of Pastoral* (London, 1935; reprint, New York: New Directions, 1960), p. 255.

10. See "The Supernatural Passage of Time in Fairyland" in Katherine M. Briggs, *The Vanishing People: Fairy Lore and Legends* (New York: Pantheon Books, 1978), pp. 11-26.

11. Brian Froud and Alan Lee, *Faeries* (New York: Harry N. Abrams, 1978), pp. 24-25.

12. See Ernest Schanzer, "The Moon and the Fairies in *A Midsummer Night's Dream,*" *University of Toronto Quarterly,* 24 (1955): 234-46.

13. The entire question of children's attendance at the public theaters seems irresolvable given the dearth of solid evidence. In the standard study of the subject, *Shakespeare's Audience* (New York: Columbia Univ. Press, 1941), Alfred Harbage seems of two minds. He first notes that "About 20 percent of the metropolitan population was under ten years of age, about 30 percent under sixteen years of age. A few children would have been taken to the theatres by their parents, but it is doubtful if many could have commanded both the freedom and the penny that would make them independent playgoers" (p. 79). He goes on to discuss the large class of

London apprentices, however, who "had no income except what spending money was allowed them by parents or masters, and theoretically they had no weekday leisure, but by hook or crook they flocked to the theatres" (p. 81). Finally, Harbage goes on to quote from Stephen Gosson's *Playes Confuted in Fiue Actions* (1582) his observation that "the common people which resorte to Theatres being but an assemblie of Tailers, Tinkers, Cordwayners, Saylers, olde Men, young Men, Women, Boyes, Girles, and such like" (p. 84) and the well-known lines from the prologue to *Every Man in His Humor* (1598): "He rather prayes, you will be pleas'd to see/ One such, to day, as other playes should be./ Where neither Chorus wafts you ore the seas,/ Nor creaking throne comes downe the boyes to please" (p. 81). It seems incontestable then that children got to the public theater by whatever means; their numbers, however, must remain conjectural. And in regard to *A Midsummer Night's Dream*, its premiere performance, at a country house, would have been witnessed by all those in the wedding party, including children.

14. C.L. Barber, *Shakespeare's Festive Comedy: A Study of Dramatic Form and Its Relation to Social Customs* (Princeton, New Jersey: Princeton University Press, 1959), p. 145. Thomas McFarland, in *Shakespeare's Pastoral Comedy* (Chapel Hill: University of North Carolina Press, 1972), also explores the ramifications of pastoralization in the play.

15. Schanzer, "The Moon and the Fairies," p. 137.

16. Barber, *Shakespeare's Festive Comedy*, p. 145.

17. Most modern critics agree with W.W. Greg's contention in *Pastoral Poetry and Pastoral Drama* (London: A.H. Bullen, 1906) that the steady contrast between two ways of life constitutes the chief constant element in the pastoral genre. The criticism implicit in this contrast is so marked that many scholars, such as Hallet Smith in *Elizabethan Poetry: A Study in Conventions, Meaning and Expression* (Cambridge, Mass.: Harvard Univ. Press, 1966), are inclined to see the pastoral mode as generically satiric.

18. As a country spirit, Puck had a strong distaste for city life, and when he found himself in the court or city, he usually regretted it, as in Ben Jonson's masque *Love Restored* (printed 1616): "Are these your court-sports! would I had kept mee to my gamboles o' the

countrey still, selling of fish, short seruice, shooing the wild mare, or rosting of ROBBIN red-brest. These were better. . . . I haue recouer'd my selfe, now, for you, I am the honest plaine countrey spirit, and harmelesse: ROBBIN goodfellow, hee that sweepes the harth, and the house cleane, riddles for the countrey maides, and does all their other drudgerie, while they are at hot-cockles: one, that ha's discours'd with your court spirits, e're now; but was faine to night to run a thousand hazards to arriue at this place; neuer poore goblin was so put to his shifts, to get in, to see nothing." *Ben Jonson*, eds. C.H. Herford and Percy and Evelyn Simpson, (Oxford: Claredon Press, 1941), 7:378-79.

19. Lord Spencer's desire to present the Queen with a jewel might also help account for the choice of a fairy entertainment, as M.W. Latham explains: "It was the fairies' well-known generosity with precious stones and other presents that made them so invaluable to generous but shrewd courtiers who wished to present a gift to Elizabeth and her successor without laying themselves liable to a suspicion of bribery. Again and again the fairies were impersonated to make the presentation of diamond or a ruby for an aspiring mortal" (*The Elizabethan Fairies*, p. 143).

20. *Ben Jonson*, 8:124.

21. The term is coined by Katherine M. Briggs in *The Anatomy of Puck*, p. 58.

22. *Works of Michael Drayton*, 3:140.

23. Floris Delattre reprints the entire 1635 anthology as Appendix I of *English Fairy Poetry.*

24. *English Poetry*, pp. 203-04.

25. *Seventeenth Century Studies* (London: K. Paul, Trench and Co., 1883), p. 131.

26. *English Fairy Poetry*, p. 209.

27. *Ibid.*, pp. 213-14.

28. *Ibid.*, p. 191.

8. The Water-Poet

1. Aside from his own pamphlets, biographical information on Taylor may be found in the *DNB* and in a biocritical essay in Wal-

lace Notestein's *Four Worthies* (New Haven: Yale University Press, 1957).

2. Margaret Spufford, *Small Books and Pleasant Histories: Popular Fiction and Its Readership in Seventeenth-Century England* (Athens: University of Georgia Press, 1982), p. 258.

3. Louis Wright, *Middle-Class Culture in Elizabethan England* (Ithaca, N.Y.: Cornell University Press, 1935); H.S. Bennett, *English Books and Readers, 1475 to 1557*, 2nd edition (Cambridge University Press, 1969) and *English Books and Readers, 1558 to 1603* (Cambridge University Press, 1965).

4. Spufford, "Elementary Education and the Acquisition of Reading Skills," in *Small Books and Pleasant Histories*, pp. 19-44. Spufford's argument is not new, but her analysis is more thorough and cogent than earlier studies which had advanced the same proposition, such as J.W. Adamson, "Literacy in England in the Fifteenth and Sixteenth Centuries," *The Library*, 4th series, 10, 2 (Sept., 1929), pp. 163-193 (rpt. in *The Illiterate Anglo-Saxon* [Cambridge, 1946]). See also the studies by R.S. Schofield, "The Measurement of Literacy in Pre-Industrial England," in *Literacy in Traditional Societies* (Cambridge, 1968), ed. J.R. Goody, and "Illiteracy in Pre-Industrial England: The Work of the Cambridge Group for the History of Population and Social Structure," in *Literacy and Society in a Historical Perspective* (1973), ed. E. Johansson.

5. See especially the important study by Philip J. Greven, *The Protestant Temperament: Patterns of Child-Rearing, Religious Experience and the Self in Early America* (New York: Knopf, 1977).

6. For a study of Taylor's travel pamphlets, see Warren W. Wooden, "The Peculiar Peregrinations of John Taylor the Water-Poet: A Study in Seventeenth-Century British Travel Literature," *Prose Studies* 6, 1 (May 1983): 3-20.

7. See E.H. Miller, *The Professional Writer in Elizabethan England* (Cambridge: Harvard University Press, 1959), pp. 164-67, for a consideration of Taylor's subscription publishing activities.

8. According to R.B. McKerrow, "it seems to be generally agreed that for the early part of the seventeenth century it is not unreasonable . . . to take 1,000 as representing an average edition.

Popular books were likely to be printed in large numbers, 1,250 or 1,500 to the edition, but books of a heavier kind might well run to only 500" ("Edward Allde as a Typical Trade Printer," *The Library,* 4th series, 10, 2 [September 1929], pp. 121-62). For example, Taylor relates that he collected over 1600 signatures on his bills before contracting with a printer for a press run of 4500 copies of *The Pennyles Pilgrimage* in 1618. See Wooden, "The Peculiar Peregrinations," pp. 8-9.

9. See, for example, Phoebe Sheavyn, *The Literary Profession in the Elizabethan Age* (New York: Haskell House, 1964; orig., 1909), pp. 85-86.

10. See Brockman, "Robin Hood and the Invention of Children's Literature," and "Children and the Audiences of Robin Hood." The classic case study of this transformation of medieval romance from the reading matter of the aristocracy to the stuff of the nursery is R.S. Crane, "The Vogue of *Guy of Warwick* from the Close of the Middle Ages to the Romantic Revival," *PMLA* 30 (1915): 125-94.

11. Spufford, *Small Books and Pleasant Histories,* p. 72.

12. As an example of the schoolboy traffic in adventure chapbooks, Margaret Spufford cites the testimony of Francis Kirkman, who in 1673 wrote of his reading tastes and habits as a schoolboy earlier in the century: "Once I happened upon a Six Pence, and having lately read that famous Book, of the *Fryar and the Boy,* and being hugely pleased with that, as also the excellent History of the *Seven wise Masters of Rome,* and having heard great commendation of *Fortunatus,* I laid out all my mony for that, and thought I had a great bargain . . . now having read this Book, and being desirous of reading more of that nature; one of my School-fellows lent me *Doctor Faustus,* which also pleased me, especially when he travelled in the Air, saw all the World, and did what he listed. . . . The next Book I met with was *Fryar Bacon,* whose pleasant Stories much delighted me: But when I came to Knight Errantry, and reading *Montelion Knight of the Oracle,* and *Ornatus* and *Artesia,* and the famous *Parisimus;* I was contented beyond measure, and (believing all I read to be true) wished my self Squire to one of these Knights: I

proceeded on to *Palmerin of England,* and *Amadis de Gaul,* and borrowing one Book of one person, when I read it my self, I lent it to another, who lent me one of their Books; and thus robbing Peter to pay Paul, borrowing and lending from one to another, I in time had read most of these Histories. All the time I had from School, as Thursdays in the afternoon, and Saturdays, I spent in reading these Books; so that I being wholly affected to them, and reading how that *Amadis* and other Knights not knowing their Parents, did in time prove to be Sons of Kings and great Personages; I had such a fond and idle Opinion, that I might in time prove to be some great Person, or at leastwise be Squire to some Knight" (p. 73).

This system of schoolboy swaps and barters for favorite chapbooks was no doubt a commonplace in seventeenth- and eighteenth-century schools. In *Tristram Shandy,* for example, Laurence Sterne has Uncle Toby recall his boyhood in the opening days of the eighteenth century with the exclamation, "When Guy, Earl of Warwick, and Parismus and Parismenus, and Valentine and Orson, and the Seven Champions of England, were handed round at school—were they not purchased with my pocket-money?" (Book 6, chapter 32).

13. These include such very diverse works as, among others, a verse elegy on the death of Prince Henry (1612), a pamphlet arguing *The True Cause of the Water-mens Suit Concerning Players* (1613), a group of satirical pamphlets poking fun at Thomas Coryat and his travel books, poetry collections, and a narrative of a sea engagement between the British "Dolphin" and six Turkish men-of-war (1616).

14. In *A Bibliography of the Thumb Bibles of John Taylor (The Water Poet)* (Aberdeen: at the University Press, 1910), p. 2, William Johnston reports that the term first appears in print in the 1849 reprint of Taylor's work by Longman and Company; Ruth E. Adomeit speculates that the use of the term at this time may have been suggested by the 1844 visit to England of P.T. Barnum's Gen. Tom Thumb. (*Three Centuries of Thumb Bibles: A Checklist* [N.Y.: Garland Publishing Co., 1980], p. xiii).

15. Brockman, "Robin Hood and the Invention of Children's Literature," p. 1.

16. Egoff, *Republic of Childhood*.

17. A.S.W. Rosenbach, *Books and Bidders: The Adventures of a Bibliophile* (Boston: Little, Brown, 1927), p. 205.

18. Ruth MacDonald, *Literature for Children in England and America from 1646 to 1774* (Troy, N.Y.: Whitston, 1982), p. 20. MacDonald also notes the use of such catch-phrases as "Penned in Metre for the great Delight and better Remembrance of the Reader" and a "Short easy and Instructional Manner" in eighteenth-century editions of Taylor's thumb Bible; these phrases, she notes, are also "frequently found in the titles of eighteenth-century children's books" (p. 20). See also Jerome Griswold, "Early American Children's Literature: A Bibliographie Primer," *Early American Literature* 18 (1983): 119-26.

19. *Salvator Mundi* (London, 1616), Sig. [A6].

20. MacDonald, *Literature for Children*, p. 18.

21. Adomeit, *Three Centuries*, p. xxxvii.

22. Louis B. Wright, for example, cites the denunciation of popularizers added by A.H. to John Davies' *A Scourge for Paper-Persecutors* (1625) in *Middle-Class Culture in Elizabethan England*, p. 98.

23. One reason for the comparative lack of success of the *Book of Martyrs* may well have been the lack of pictures in Taylor's edition. The absence of illustrations did not interfere with the appreciation of the Bible, but the electrifying pictures of suffering martyrs had been a major part of the attraction of Foxe's book, especially for young readers. See chapter 5.

24. *Sir Gregory Nonsence His Newes from no place . . .* (London, [1622]), Sig. A4-[A5v]. Page references for subsequent quotations are included in the text.

25. G.K. Chesterton's distinction between the spirit of nonsense and that of satire is relevant here: "It is true in a certain sense that some of the greatest writers the world has seen—Aristophanes, Rabelais and Sterne—have written nonsense; but unless we are mistaken, it is in a widely different sense. The nonsense of these men was satiric—that is to say, symbolic; it was a kind of exuberant capering round a discovered truth. There is all the difference in the world between the instinct of satire, which, seeing in the Kaiser's moustaches something typical of him, draws them continually larger and larger; and the instinct of nonsense which, for no reason

whatever, imagines what those moustaches would look like on the present Archbishop of Canterbury if he grew them in a fit of absence of mind." "A Defense of Nonsense," in *The Man Who Was Chesterton,* ed. Raymond T. Bond (New York: Dodd, Mead, 1945), pp. 605-06. Taylor returned to nonsense verse late in his career with *Nonsense upon Sence, or Sence upon Nonsence* and *The Essence, Quintessence, Insence, Innocence, Lye-sence, & Magnifisence of Nonsence upon Sence* in the early 1650s. A strong royalist, during the conflict of the 1640s Taylor had turned out a number of anti-Puritan satires. Under a Puritan government in the 1650s, he was only a little more circumspect, using a veneer of nonsense in these two pamphlets to launch yet another attack on religious sectaries. Thus, neither pamphlet qualifies by Chesterton's distinction as the type of "pure" nonsense associated with the best nonsense verse for children and found in *Sir Gregory Nonsence.*

26. *A Dog of War* (London: Frederick Etchells and Hugh Mac-Donald, 1927). This limited edition, "with hand-coloured Engravings on wood by Hester Sainsbury," was apparently intended as a coffee-table book for dog lovers. Although based on a chapbook copy in the Bodleian, this edition modernizes Taylor's language and spelling, and both his prose preface and concluding survey of faithful animals since antiquity "have been omitted as being dull."

27. *A Dogge of Warre, or The Trauels of Drunkard, the famous Curre of the Round Woollstaple in Westminster. His seruices in the Netherlands, and lately in FRANCE, with his home returne* in *All the Workes of Iohn Taylor the Water-Poet Comprised in the Folio Edition of 1630* (Manchester: Spenser Society, 1869), p. 366. Future quotations refer to this edition with page numbers included in the text.

28. Cf. Victor E. Neuburg: "The customary price of chapbooks in the early 17th century was one penny each." (*Chapbooks* [London: Vine Press, 1964], p. 1.

9. Nature Moralized

1. John Bunyan, *A Book for Boys and Girls; Or, Country Rhymes for Children.* A Facsimilie of the Unique First Edition Published in 1686.

Deposited in the British Museum. Introduction by John Brown (New York: A.C. Armstrong and Son, n.d. [1860?]).

2. For a discussion of the versions of Bunyan's book, see the introduction to *John Bunyan's A Book for Boys and Girls Or Country Rhymes for Children*, ed. E.S. Buchanan (New York: American Tract Society, 1928).

3. *John Bunyan: The Poems*, ed. Graham Midgley, vol. 6 of *The Miscellaneous Works of John Bunyan*, ed. Roger Sharrock (Oxford: Clarenden Press, 1980), xliii.

4. Rosemary Freeman, *English Emblem Books* (New York: Octagon Books, 1966), 214.

5. See Freeman, *English Emblem Books*; Roger Sharrock, "John Bunyan and the English Emblem Writers," *Review of English Studies* 21, 82 (April, 1945); Lynn V. Sadler, *John Bunyan* (Boston: Twayne, 1979).

6. On the other hand, lack of system and order has been assumed, for example, by Ola Elizabeth Winslow in *John Bunyan* (New York: Macmillan, 1961): "There is no logic back of [Bunyan's] choice of subjects, any more than in what by chance arrests the quick interest of a child. The charm is in the unexpectedness of a subject and the simple literalness of the jingling couplet" (p. 192).

7. See Milo Kaufmann, *The Pilgrim's Progress and Traditions in Puritan Meditations* (New Haven: Yale Univ. Press, 1968).

Bibliography

Primary

Babee's Book, The (ca. 1475)

Bunyan, John. *A Book for Boys and Girls: or, Country Rhimes for Children* (1686)

———. *The Pilgrim's Progress* (1678)

Caxton, William. *Book of Curtesye* (1477)

———. *Fables of Aesop* (1483)

———. *Reynard the Fox* (1481)

Chaucer, Geoffrey. *A Treatise on the Astrolabe* (1391)

Comenius, John Amos. *Orbis Sensualium Pictus* (1657), trans. Charles Hoole (1658)

Drayton, Michael. *Nymphidia, the Court of Faery* (1627)

Erasmus, Desiderius. *De ciuilitate morum puerilium: A lytell booke of good manners for children* (1532), trans. Robert Whittington

Janeway, James. *A Token for Children* (1672)

Jole, William. *The Father's Blessing* (1674)

Knight of the Tower, The (1484)

Malory, Sir Thomas. *Le Morte D'Artur* (1485)

Pyson, Richard. *Guy of Warwick* (ca. 1520)

Rhodes, Hugh. *Boke of Nurture* (1545)

Rimbault, Edward F., ed. *Two Sermons Preached By the Boy Bishop.* Camden Society Miscellany. Vol. 7 (Westminster: Camden Society, 1875)

Robin Goodfellow; His Mad Pranks and Merry Jests (1628)

S., R. *A Description of the King and Queene of Fayries, their habit, fare, their abode, pompe, and state* (1635). Reprinted as appendix in Delattre.

Seager, Francis. *The Schoole of Vertue and Booke of good Hourture for Chyldren to learn theyr Dutie by* (1557)

Skelton, John. *Hereafter foloweth the Boke of Phyllip Sparowe* (ca. 1545)

Taylor, John. *A Dogge of Warre* (1628)

————. *Nonsence Upon Sence, or Sence Upon Nonsence* (ca. 1653)

White, Thomas. *A Little Book for Little Children* (1674)

Wynken de Worde. *A Lytell Geste of Robin Hode* (ca. 1500)

Foxe, John. *Book of Martyrs* (1563)

Secondary

Aries, Philippe. *Centuries of Childhood: A Social History of Family Life.* New York: Alfred Knopf, 1967.

Brockman, B.A. "Children and the Audiences of Robin Hood," *South Atlantic Review* 48, No. 2 (1983) 67-83.

————. "Robin Hood and the Invention of Children's Literature," *Children's Literature* 10 (1982) 1-17.

Crane, R. S. "The Vogue of *Guy of Warwick* from the Close of the Middle Ages to the Romantic Revival," *PMLA* 30 (1915) 125-94.

Darton, F. J. Harvey. *Children's Books in England: Five Centuries of Social Life.* Cambridge: Cambridge University Press, 1958), Ed. 2.

Davidson, E. W. "*Orbis Pictus:* Comenius' Contributions to Children's Literature," unpublished dissertation, Catholic University of America, 1958.

Delattre, Floris. *English Fairy Poetry: From the Origins to the Seventeenth Century.* London: Henry Frowde, 1912.

Demers, Patricia, and Gordon Moyles, eds. *From Instruction to Delight: An Anthology of Children's Literature to 1850.* Toronto: Oxford University Press, 1982.

De Molen, Richard L. "*Pueri Christi Imitatio:* The Festival of the Boy-Bishop in Tudor England," *Moreana* 45 (1975) 17-28.

Egoff, Sheila. *The Republic of Childhood.* Oxford: Oxford University Press, 1967.

Gillespie, Margaret C. *Literature for Children: History and Trends.* Dubuque, Iowa: W.C. Brown, 1970.

Griffith, John W., and Charles H. Frey, eds. *Classics of Children's Literature.* New York: Macmillan, 1981.

Hale, David G. "Aesop in Renaissance England," *The Library* 27 (1972) 116-25.

Hodnett, Edward. *Aesop in England: The Transmission of Motifs in Seventeenth-Century Illustrations of Aesop's Fables.* Charlottesville: University Press of Virginia, 1979.

Latham, Minor W. *The Elizabethan Fairies.* Reprinted, New York: Octagon Books, 1972.

MacDonald, Ruth. *Literature for Children in England and America from 1646 to 1774.* Troy, New York: Whitston Publishing Co., 1982.

Marcus, Leah Sinanoglou. *Childhood and Cultural Despair: A Theme and Variations in Seventeenth-Century Literature.* Pittsburgh: University of Pittsburgh Press, 1979.

Miner, Robert G., Jr. "Aesop as Litmus: The Acid Test of Children's Literature," *Children's Literature* 1 (1972) 9-15.

Muir, Percival H. *English Children's Books, 1600-1900.* London: Batsford, 1954.

Pinchbeck, Ivy, and Margaret Hewitt. *Children in English Society.* Volume 1 of *From Tudor Times to the 18th Century.* London: Routledge & Kegan Paul, 1969.

Sloane, William. *Children's Books in England and America in the Seventeenth Century.* New York: Columbia University Press, 1955.

Smith, Lillian H. *The Unreluctant Years: A Critical Approach to Children's Literature.* Chicago: American Library Association, 1953.

Spufford, Margaret. *Small Books and Pleasant Histories: Popular Fiction and Its Readership in Seventeenth-Century England.* Athens, Ga.: University of Georgia Press, 1982.

Stone, Lawrence W. *The Family, Sex and Marriage in England, 1500-1800.* New York: Harper and Row, 1977.

Sutherland, Zena, and May Hill Arbuthnot. *Children and Books.* Glenview, Illinois: Scott Foresman, 1977. Edition 5.

Thwaite, Mary F. *From Primer to Pleasure in Reading: An Introduction to the History of Children's Books in England.* London: Library Association, 1963.

Wooden, Warren W. "Early English Children's Literature: A Report," *The Children's Literature Association Quarterly* 5, No. 1 (1980) 12-14.

———. "More Children's Literature Studies in the Carolinas," *The Children's Literature Association Quarterly* 6, No. 1 (1981) 8.

———. Review of John W. Griffith and Charles H. Frey, eds., *Classics of Children's Literature,* and of Patricia Demers and Gordon Moyles, eds., *From Instruction to Delight* in *The Children's Literature Association Quarterly* 7, No. 3 (1982) 62-63.

———. Review of Leah Sinanoglou Marcus, *Childhood and Cultural Despair* in *The Journal of Psychohistory* 7 (1979) 371-74.

Index